Man of Sorrows

& Sorrow

The woes, warmth and wonder of Jesus

dave@davehopwood.com

A very big thankyou to Martin Purnell for all his help and proofreading.

The back cover image features the decorated cross in the chapel at the Lee Abbey community in Devon. A photograph taken in September 2002. Lee Abbey is a beautiful place which has been life-changing in so many ways for me.

Part 1:
Running on Water

Snatches

Imagine the scene, Simon Peter, that big fisherman from Galilee, is pacing and talking, talking and pacing, moving his arms as he speaks, making shapes and punching the air as he presses home the stories he's telling. A younger, smaller guy in the corner, is scribbling away, missing words and dropping letters as he tries to keep up. There's nothing calm or dignified about the scene. Life drips from the stories, like sweat from the storyteller. On and on and on, tales of encounters and arguments, miracles and murder. A hillside littered with chewing people, a rocky outcrop triple-speared by three crosses and three men bleeding to death. And two gardens, one shrouded in shadows and betrayal, the other bathed in the new dawn light, as angels leap out from tombs, and a gardener waits to surprise a broken-hearted friend. And these are just glimpses, just snatches of what the big fisherman is saying. Pouring out the globe-moulding odyssey he has lived through for three years.

Seething-with-life

I'm not sure that a book like this can truly capture the essence/reality/wonder/pain/laughter/fully-human-and-sublimely-divine nature of Jesus from Nazareth. Perhaps it's just plain foolhardy to try, but here's my attempt anyway. I hope it'll be helpful and make sense, and I hope it'll be grammatically correct, or at least come close to that. Mind you, for years I thought 'because' was spelt *'becouse'*, so we can only hope. I hope there'll be some surprises too.

Some might say it's better to just pick up a Bible and read that. I love the gospels and there is no doubt that the best way to encounter Jesus in page form is to open up that profound, startling, seething-with-life Good Book and start reading the breathtaking verses that Mark has scribbled down for us. It's widely thought that Mark was recording Peter's narrated accounts and at times it feels as if it was a challenge for him to keep up with the big fisherman, as he spilled his story.

Side Doors

So all of that said, I guess what I can do is try and come at all that from a side door, through a little used fire-exit, and do my best to add a few extra splashes of paint to what Mark and the other first-century writers have written. Their words come at us loaded with grit and glory. And infused with the DNA of the Holy Spirit. I can't compete with that.

I'll be using lots of stories and creative bits, because, well, why not? Better to offer things in an open-handed style for you to chew on and think about. This is what Jesus did, so how can I not follow that way? (Plus I love stories. So that's most probably the real reason!) You may find that some of these thoughts and tales seem random, and you have to join the dots for yourself. Also certain stories get repeated and revisited. This is deliberate. We often need to hear something a few times for it to start setting us thinking. (That's my excuse anyway.)

Misunderstood

There have been three occasions where people have been shocked/bemused/horrified/taken aback by the sudden loudness of my 'I know how to stage project' voice. Once when I was working on a training exercise in a theatre, and we were told to ask an imaginary audience to leave the auditorium due to an imaginary fire. Secondly when we were trying to move a group of sheep from one field to another. (Let's face it, sheep take a lot of moving). And thirdly at a wedding when I was trying to herd guests from one location to another, and no one really realised I was the best man, and that it was this best man's job to yell at them. On all three occasions I recall the perplexed, bemused looks and the take-a-step-back recoiling. These recollections make me flinch when I remember them, and I still feel the reaction was a tad unfair. I mean, people should expect me to boom if you ask me to do that, tell me to issue a command and I'll come out with all tonsils blazing. So to form a tenuous link… I'm sure that Jesus often wrongfooted people. I'd like to have been a fly on the wall when the booming of his actions and the unexpected nature of his stories and miracles made jaws drop, eyes widen and bodies recoil. I think he must have garnered that startled reaction regularly. In a way that he doesn't seem to now. We often talk about walking on water, or turning water to wine, and yet don't stagger a little into the furniture as we say these things.

Exhausted

In Nick Hornby's novel *How to be Good*, he describes the experience of a stranger going to Sunday church when she'd only ever been to weddings and funerals before. In his words she'd 'never been to a bog-standard, nobody-there service'.

And she describes it like this – 'it feels sad, exhausted, defeated; this may have been God's house once... but he's clearly moved on, gone to a place where there is more a demand for this sort of thing.' I'm always interested in the experiences and descriptions of folk who are not used to church. And this sounds very depressing indeed. Presumably Nick Hornby must have been to weary services like this himself in order to write about one. Now clearly there are many churches in which the Sunday services are way livelier than this. And I don't mind small quiet services myself these days. But I get the point. We're in the territory of the dry predictability of organised religion here. The very fact that churches have 'orders of service' kind of gives it away, doesn't it. Now don't get me wrong, the synagogues Jesus went to would have had a certain order to them, but Jesus often cooked up a bit of a storm when he went to organised events. Think of his table-turning in the temple, his winemaking at that wedding, and those times of going to the synagogue when he upset the important folk in charge by (shock horror!) daring to help and healing people.

Reverence

I want to take a moment to consider how we read the Bible in public. For much of my life I've been an Anglican, though I do speak in churches of various denominations in my work these days. But for a lot of the services I go to, after the Bible reading the usual response is this – the reader: 'This is the word of the Lord', then us: 'Thanks be to God.' Now I understand the reason for this, I get the desire for respect and reverence, and a willingness to receive the word of God, but, well... it just seems too tidy, too ordered. When folk heard Jesus's teaching and stories – their eyes popped. Or they heckled him. Or their jaws dropped. Or they said things like 'Seriously?' Amazement, wonder, questions, shock, gasps and doubletakes rippled through the crowd. When was the last time you gasped at a Bible reading?

Hand to Mouth

One that might have you reacting a little is the incredible account of Ehud and Eglon, in that fierce thriller known as Judges 3 vv 12–30. This is an eye-watering account of gruesome detail, and the one time I asked someone to read it in a church service there were audible reactions to it. Judges is a brutal book which shows the futility of violence. The Judges or Governors rise and fall and the people continue on a destructive cycle. They live their own way, things fall apart, they come running back to God, he sends them a judge, and the people wander off again. I read somewhere that the period of the Judges takes place because Joshua never appointed a successor. And so for a while there was a kind of oh-yes-we-need-God/oh-no-we-don't existence, a sort of spiritual hand to mouth kind of life.

Engagement

Just last night I was sailing with Paul on his action-packed adventure through Acts 21. In verse 4 we're told that some believers in Tyre prophesied in the Holy Spirit that Paul shouldn't go to Jerusalem. And yet he still went. Really? A message came from the Holy Spirit and Paul did the opposite? What's going on? Why did Paul not listen? Not long after a prophet called Agabus (great name) tied himself in knots with Paul's belt, just to show what would happen to the great evangelist. It's a smorgasbord of warnings here.

But you see what I mean? The story begs questions, it draws them out of me. It's certainly the word of the Lord, and I thank God for it, but I want a bit of liturgy that goes, 'You're kidding aren't you? Why would that happen?' And I'm not expressing doubt here (though doubt is a key part of faith), I just want to do what the writers of the Bible call us to do, have an engagement with God's word that involves more than a tidy one-liner. I mean, can you imagine Goliath swearing at the Israelites and then David fore-heading him with a killer stone, and the Israelites nodding politely and saying, 'This is the word of the Lord.' Just as the blood starts draining from the giant's severed head and pooling round their feet.

Six Days

We can also reduce the wondrous nature of biblical narrative to arguments about belief and proof. There is much debate, for example, about whether God managed to make the world in six real days, or six poetic days, or six figurative days, or six evolutionary days, or six light year days. Ignoring the fact that God is outside of time anyway, and only invented time on the fourth 'day'. I like to think that the first day lasted 100 million years, the second a thousand light years, the third twenty minutes, the fourth fifteen seconds, the fifth a decade, and the sixth a leisurely coffee break, the length of your own choosing. And then God thought, 'Right – let's see them work that lot out! Explain that!' If nothing else it reminds me that our understanding is always going to be much smaller than God's and secondly that God has the biggest sense of humour in the universe.

To frame a question in a way that Jesus might well have asked… (check out Mark 2 v 9) Is it easier to create a world in seven days, or to design a universe out of love and the desire for good friendship and company?

Controversial

Just to be controversial for a moment, our liturgy and bible reading, rather than retelling the story of our faith and life in an exuberant and extraordinary God, can at times sound more like reading terms and conditions. I can only speak for myself here and say that it's easy for me to fall into the trap of rapidly reciting that which is required, or important to know. Rather than being revitalised and reinvigorated by the great story of faith in which we find ourselves. Once, when I worked and lived at the Lee Abbey conference centre in North Devon, we celebrated the biblical festival of shelters by constructing a makeshift shelter, wood, fruit, branches an' all. Some folk wielded drills and screwdrivers, others knitted branches together, some got involved with the decorations, and the rest sat around chatting and watching. It was probably the best example I have had of living the story. Finding myself in the Good Book. Rather than having a church service with hymns and readings and a talk, we reconstructed what the Israelites did as they crossed the desert, escaping slavery and brutality.

Reliving

When we relive the last supper in most churches we have a communion prayer of some sort, but this can seem a little dry at times. Rather than experiencing this tale of slaves freed in Egypt, and ourselves being freed each Sunday morning as we celebrate this meal, rather than being caught up in this great adventure of escape, we find ourselves traipsing through familiar words, perhaps joining in on cue, merely to get to the moment when we will receive the bread and wine in some form. Or even worse, (to be confessional for a moment) to reach the end of the service. Rather than taking time to breathlessly escape into the life being offered as we discover again the unending dangerous grace of God. Daily bible reading can be the same too. Now of course it would be exhausting to truly enter into the drama of these stories every time we open a Bible or join in with liturgy. But it's just a plea for more dynamic engagement at times.

3D

A good friend of mine recently commented on Bible reading, pointing out that it can sometimes sound a little flat, as there are no stage directions. We aren't told about tone of voice used, or facial expression, or body language displayed as the various characters are speaking. Jon described it as being a little like looking at the satellite image on Google earth, when we look straight down and we can see that all the information is there. But when we hit 3D view, we can see the satellite view from an angle and we can see the world in relief, with the various heights and dips and shapes. Often, watching the Bible portrayed as in the recent series *The Chosen,* or in other films and series, it is a little like reading the Bible in 3D. We see more colour and shade, realise the characters are real people, three dimensional with back stories and fears, ambitions, and dreams. I hope there may be moments in this book when another dimension appears as you revisit some of these stories.

Guts Ache

We need to let the Bible get to us. To get inside us. To respect and honour it by chewing on it. The danger of reading bits we already know and agree with is that we close it again having not had a proper conversation with it. When we saunter into the first chapter of Ezekiel we find he is given the word of God in a scroll – and then he's told to eat it! Yes! Really! He's to munch on it, let it swill around his mouth, get a few bits stuck in his teeth, then swallow and digest it, be surprised by the flavour and the texture. And no doubt some of the bits that got wedged in his teeth will slip free later for him to chew on some more. John, the Revelation guy, is given a scroll at the end of chapter nine of his big screen epic. When he eats this one it tastes good in his mouth, but it then gives him guts ache!

Feast

These living words are not always easy to digest, we can take a while to adjust to the diet. Plus not everything in there is good for us and sanctioned by God. Little Gideon starts well in Judges 6 but ends up on a killing spree two chapters later. Esther saves her people from annihilation only for them to get rather over-excited by the sound of swishing swords and move from defence to attack. Leap into Judges 11 (I'd wear a crash helmet if I were you, it's dangerous in there) and you encounter the awful tale of Jephthah's daughter. Her dad makes a rash vow, to sacrifice whatever comes out of his house to greet him when he gets home. What was he expecting? The cat? A stream of cockroaches? A Cornish pasty? Well… it's his young daughter, of course it is. She's seen her daddy through the window and wants to give him a hug. Whether she is actually sacrificed or instead lives as an unmarried virgin all her life remains a debated outcome. But the point is there. Jephthah didn't have to make that vow. It was a huge mistake. God draws us into a covenant, an agreement and a relationship that he makes. He makes his vow to us, based on grace and truth, compassion and understanding. The sacrifice he invites is of our whole life, the good and the bad bits, the raw material of our daily living.

Rush back to Genesis chapter 4 and we find a guy called Lamech marrying two women, at the same time. Thus paving the way for a whole raft of polygamy. So many men marrying so many women all at once I doubt any raft would stay afloat. Gideon didn't have to turn into the Terminator. Lamech didn't need a wife on each arm. These things were not the best plan, far from it. And we're invited to read and wrestle and chew and debate. To eat the scroll and let it taste sweet and then give us stomach ache. For a while, until we find another scroll that maybe tastes unusual but then turns out be a satisfying and hearty feast.

Egyptian Chariots

King Solomon's an interesting guy, because early on in his reign, in 1 Kings chapter 3, he is given the gift of wisdom, and he knows how to share it. Plunder the riches of Proverbs and you'll have plenty to chew on for a lifetime. However, read on in 1 Kings and we find a guy who does not always live wisely. He built a fine temple for God, but he also built a mighty fine palace for himself. And he used forced labour. Yes, slaves. He also acquired weaponry, horses and chariots. Some of them from Egypt. Egyptian chariots? Forced labour? Isn't that a tad contrary to an old story in which Moses was sent by God to set slaves free? Hmm. And now here's the king of Israel, enslaving others. Wise or unwise? You decide. And if you want an example of someone following in Lamech's footsteps… well, 300 wives and 700 concubines. I rest my case. He's a fine example of the way it's often easier to talk the talk rather than walk the walk. We can all identify with that. But I'm wandering way off the point here. We need to get back to a king who did not need a palace or armaments. Which, by the way, is what Jesus is referring to when he says – foxes (King Herod) have holes (a palace), birds of the air (the Romans) have nests (fortresses), but the son of man has nowhere to lay his head. He doesn't need weapons, or pompous establishments. Down with the people is where he chooses to be.

Reducing

It's tempting to reduce following Jesus to rules, regulations and attending church meetings. But that's surely a bit like turning the Mona Lisa into painting by numbers. You know, join the dots and you'll have a masterpiece. It'll all make sense for you. And yet… as we read the stories of Jesus we find that the dots meander all over the place. On two occasions Jesus fed thousands with a packed lunch, yet we are told in Luke chapter 8 that he and his followers were financially supported by a group of female disciples. On other occasions he went to the house of his close friends Mary and Martha for a meal. Why? Couldn't Jesus have fed them all every day with the same miracle? Well apparently not. The path meanders. Mary and Martha feeding them was just a different sort of miracle I guess. So too the women sacrificially supporting him. And these things are the same today.

Parables

Parables and stories invite comment and comeback. The best modern parables I have encountered recently have been episodes of *Black Mirror* on Netflix. And I'm certainly not recommending them. They are startling, unpleasant and in bad taste. And unforgettable. But that's the thing, once you have seen them you cannot easily dismiss them, and to me that's what a parable should be. It doesn't need to be in bad taste, but it should be more than a simple tale one can agree with or applaud or sidestep before ousting it from our minds. Parables should annoy us or uplift us or startle and affect us to the point we will never forget them. And therefore they may not be nice. They may be annoying. Or disturbing. And they may get the teller in trouble. After all the prophets frequently used sex as a metaphor. Heard anything like that in church lately? 'You're like donkeys on heat at mating time, sniffing the wind for a mate!' Jeremiah yelled, in chapter 2 of his startling epic. I'm not sure my stories and creative pieces will be as arresting. But hopefully they will be thought-provoking.

Imagining

The poem *Running on Water* is inspired by a conversation I had with our older daughter Amy, whilst we were out on a meandering walk. I think I was lamenting the way that things become unremarkable to us, so the phrases 'walking on water' and 'water into wine' are now used willy-nilly, and do not hold for us the wonder and laughter and exuberance that they might well have had for those first friends of Jesus. So we began to imagine what it might have been like if Jesus had run across the water, and done other things too. Things that might almost seem heretical to imagine... and so here's my attempted heretical scribble...

Running on Water

I suppose you didn't need only to walk
On that raging splashy unsupportive chaotic restless stuff.
But could have run a marathon on it,
Or broken the 100m Olympic record.
Or hopped and skipped and jumped,
Or sped with an egg and spoon,
Or bounced in a hessian sack,
Or water-skied... without the skies... or the speedboat.

I suppose you didn't need to stop at wine,
You could have made beer,
Or champagne or prosecco or sherry,
Or gin and tonic, or vodka martini...
Shaken not stirred, of course.
Lemonade, Fanta, milk shakes, slushies, and iced tea.
Lots you could have made with your bursting, glad and generous heart,
As you turned an embarrassing day into a heavenly party.

I suppose you needn't have stopped at 5000,
Could have fed 10 or 15 or 20,000 or 100,000,
Or a million even, the whole world actually,
Way more than Bob Geldof and Band Aid,
But then we wouldn't have been a part of it,

15

Wouldn't have had the chance to join in.
To care and flex the muscles of our generosity.
To have our hearts and minds moved and shaped,
To have the chance to become a little more like you.

There was, however, nothing more you could have done,
Nothing more extravagant, nothing more extreme, or extraordinary,
Nothing more surprising, arresting and shocking,
As you stretched out your hands and submitted
To the will and wreckage and ways of this world.
Nothing more you could have given on that fearful Friday,
Nothing more you could have surrendered for us.
You gave it all, every ounce of energy, every last part of your being,
In order to change everything. A billion new starts offered,
In the divine and earthy crevices of your nail-pierced hands.
Nothing more. Nothing less.

Part 2:
Little Monsters

The Blame Game

Forgiving ourselves and believing that God forgives us can both be difficult concepts to hold onto, and if you're like me, it's easier to feel forgiven on days when you don't feel you have done much wrong. Harder when you are well aware of your misdemeanours and failings. The misconception of course is that we are sinners when we sin, and forgiven when we do not. But that's to miss the point. In Jesus we are forgiven sinners all the time. The biblical word is *hamartia*, which means to miss the target. To miss God's best. So it's not so much about getting things right or wrong, but rather missing out on the best kind of life God has for us. To miss the mark. *Hamartia*. Too often I imagine God as an old, fierce man with a big stick. Or perhaps a light sabre. Either way I fear he will punish me for the many things I get wrong. So with that in mind, here's a scene from John chapter 9, in which the followers of Jesus display their view of God as someone on the hunt for our mistakes, someone looking to punish rather than forgive. Jesus wrong-foots the lot of them, with a smile or two no doubt…

They want him to join in, to point out what this man has done wrong, to call him out for his mistakes and misdemeanours. To put him down so that others can big themselves up. But Jesus won't do that, he hasn't come to hcm people in, to accuse them or dismiss them, to manipulate or relegate anyone. He has come to bring hope and a light in the darkness, and welcome for those ostracised by others. To mend hearts and break chains. And so, instead of hurling accusations around, and spouting self-justifying unkindness, he smiles at the man and offers him the good news of God. He opens his eyes to a world way bigger. He brings him a new start and conjures warmth and courage. His friends look on wide-eyed themselves. This challenges their own expectations, shatters their small worldviews, and blows open their limited ideas about God. They'll never be the same again. The man meanwhile goes away, to wash the mud off his eyes and find daylight bursting upon him like a sudden flurry of a snowstorm. He wasn't perfect, far from it, but that wasn't the point. Jesus has come to bring new life, new insight and new forgiveness, and to draw us away from the darkness of judging and criticising, towards the light that sets us free to live again. He knows that compassion can coax us out of the shadows of our fear, and that a little faith, hope and love can change the world.

John 9 v 1–7

The Great Gift of Forgiveness

I recently read a great trilogy of books by author Chris Aslan. Chris reimagines various stories from the gospels, loading his tales with fistfuls of details of life at the time and in the culture of Jesus. In Mosaic, the third book in the series, he revisits the tale of the four friends lowering a man through the roof because the house where Jesus was teaching was too packed with bodies to make it in through the door. It's a great read, and in Chris's version the four young men have carried their friend on a lengthy journey through the mountains to reach Jesus. For us one of the most powerful things in that account is a man leaping up and walking again after being paralysed for years. Yet that's not the emphasis in chapter 2 of Mark's breathless account. It's not the emphasis in Luke 5 either. In both cases Jesus looks at the man and offers him the powerful gift of forgiveness. In Chris Aslan's account this makes the young man cry because of his past. And there are gasps in the room from the religious experts, those who know perfectly well, in great detail, how God operates. And it's not like this. You do not, cannot get forgiveness from a travelling preacher called Jesus in someone's home. Or in the streets. Or in the gutters. Or in the markets and shops. Or in the sports stadiums or cinemas or car parks. And so they accuse Jesus of being very wrong indeed. Of going against the ways of God. Of offending God.

And Jesus doesn't bat an eyelid. He probably smiled at those who hoped that the religious experts were wrong. Those who couldn't get to the temple for forgiveness, those who couldn't afford to pay for it, those who couldn't get clean enough to be acceptable, those who weren't well enough to be admitted into such a holy place. *Metanoia* is the word in the gospels for repent – it means change the way you think. And this was a great opportunity to do just that. Don't think God can forgive you anywhere and everywhere? Free of charge? No matter who you are or what you've done? No matter how poor or rejected you feel? Think again Buster. And so Jesus says to everyone – 'What's easier, to forgive sins, or to make a paralysed man walk?' In other words, the healing he brought into the young man's life was a sign, a sign of his power to set us free from the burden of guilt we carry. And that is very good news indeed. Extraordinarily good news. Often the guilt we feel can be over stupid mistakes, embarrassing things we dare not admit to others. Our bumbling errors make us feel small and stupid.

Little Monsters

Those critters, those cheap shots,
Those mistakes and mess-ups,
Those words we said or didn't say,
Did or didn't do,
These things that trap us and make us feel
Bad, small, wrong, or stupid.
These little monsters which settle,
Make their homes in our being,
And nag away, robbing us of hope,
Strength, peace, and well-being.
These things which seem so inconsequential,
So small, that we dare not mention them,
For fear of looking stupid, looking mad,
They hold us in check, paint us into a corner.
And so we keep them inside, bouncing off the walls
Of our brains, messing up our emotions,
As we imagine that we are the only ones
Who would ever be disturbed by such things.

Mendoza

Guilt can define so much of who we are and what we do. It can belittle us, anger us, muddy our perspective on life. It can affect how we treat others. And here comes Jesus, with his gasp-inducing ability to work a miracle – to cut us free from the burden of the past and the present. In the movie *The Mission*, Mendoza has two shadows hanging over him. He is a slave trader, and he has killed his brother, and so he carries a huge net full of his armour – the tools of his slave trading

– up a precarious waterfall. A kind of penance. He cannot let go of his past. It follows him around weighing down his every step. At the top of the waterfall a member of the tribe he has been enslaving comes at him with a knife. Will he punish Mendoza? Will he kill him now he has the chance? Will he slit his throat? There is a moment of tension, we are on the edge of our seats, what is the answer here? What is the best way forward? The man with the knife breaks into a grin, reaches round and cuts the ropes securing the net, he rolls the pile of armour away and over the cliff top. It bumps and clangs as it crashes all the way back down eventually splashing into the water. Gone forever. Mendoza laughs and cries and is hugged by his friends. He is free.

Fuel

A dear friend told me recently of an evening when he had needed to forgive a family member. As his son spoke about what had happened, and the mistake he'd made, my friend became suddenly aware of how much he had himself been forgiven by God. Out of that reminder and realisation he forgave his son. The forgiveness he had received was the fuel for forgiving someone else. That reminds me of the time a woman knelt and cried at Jesus's feet. She washed his feet and wiped them with her hair, a deeply intimate act of service. Something that would have shocked those watching. A woman letting her hair down like that in public? Unacceptable. Provocative. Appalling. But not to Jesus, he explained what she had done like this. 'A person who has been forgiven much can love much. This woman knows that she has been forgiven for her many sins, and that's why she has so much love to give.'

Mind-bending

No matter how great or small, no matter how logical or illogical, justifiable, embarrassing, or foolish our mistakes and mess-ups, Jesus understands them all. And has the power to set us free.

I recently met a lady who told me how she had forgiven someone. Day after day she had spoken her forgiveness out loud, though she had not felt it. This was a very hard thing to do. But she went on, day after day, speaking out her forgiveness. And then one day she realised. Her heart had caught up with her mind. She really had forgiven. God had worked the miracle. He had set her free.

There were two mind-bending, earth-jolting miracles that day in Mark's gospel. The miracle of the young man whose world was turned upside-down as he leapt off that stretcher, and the miracle of the forgiveness offered to all of us, those in that house, and those who of us who read it, or hear it, or watch that story retold again. The great gift of forgiveness which has the power to help us all jump up and live again.

That's the thing about Jesus's miracles – they spread far and wide. When one person gets helped – we discover we can all be helped.

- When a blind person sees – lots of eyes are opened
- When a girl is resurrected – lots of people start to live again
- When a man on a stretcher walks – lots of people get moving again
- When we see someone forgiven – we start to find forgiveness too
- When people are seen and known by Jesus, we discover he sees and knows us

Cycling

According to Rob Bell, Abraham, yes the one who struck out into the unknown in Genesis chapter 12, lived in a cynical time when everyone believed you were stuck in a cycle. Same old same old. Round and round and round. What happened to you, would happen to your children, and to their children. No chance of ever breaking out, life had painted us all into a corner. So when Abraham struck out and headed off into the unknown, following the call of an invisible God, this was unheard of. This was radical. Not least because gods were normally visible and made of stone and wood. Well, here the living God, who spoke and moved and cared, was inviting Abraham to step into a new life, to start again, to break out of the cycle. And in the chapters that follow we discover his journey. And it's a rollercoaster ride.

And here comes Jesus, then and now, inviting us to break out of the cycles that depress us, that wear us down and even sometimes trap us. Offering hope in the chaos, a light in the darkness, calm in the storms, peace in the conflict. A different way.

Two Gods (a parable of sorts)

A woman went walking in her dreams one night, and, suddenly growing wings, she was able to fly over the gulf between earth and heaven. She found herself landing on a desert road, and walking on, it wasn't long before she spotted a crooked figure, an old man with a big stick. Every so often he would jab his gnarled stick into the dirty earth and lightning bolts would flash from it.

'Who are you?' she asked.

He smiled a gap-toothed grin, but there was little warmth in it. 'I'm God,' he said.

'So… is this heaven?' she asked.

'Who said you had the right to come into heaven?' he replied.

'Well, I… I don't know…' she replied. 'I just assumed…'

'Oh did you now?' snapped the man. 'Well move a little to your left will you?'

She did and the old man waved his stick at the gap over her left shoulder. Thunder cracked and a lightning bolt flew past her. She turned to see a town on fire in the distance.

'You did that?' she asked, terror creeping through her soul.

He shrugged and grunted. Then he turned and waved his stick in the other direction. A dark cloud moved into view over a nearby city. And the rains came. In no time at all the floods had risen and the city was clearly entering a time of great distress.

'You know – you're just the way I thought you'd be,' she said.

'Really?' he said, and he held her gaze with his as he began to melt before her eyes. Before long he was little more than a pile of clothes on the floor. Imagining some kind of magic trick she crept forward and kicked at the pile.

'What are you doing that for?' said a voice.

She spun round, there was a gardener, in a patch of garden nearby. She'd not noticed him before. He smiled and there was warmth in his eyes.

'Who are you?' she asked.

'Who d'you think I might be?'

'I don't know,' she replied. 'Can you help me? I seem to be lost.'

'I'll show you the way home,' the man said. 'I'll show you other good things too.'

The gardener laid down his hoe and they began walking together.

'Who was he?' the woman asked, as they passed the pile of old clothes.

'Oh him? That was God,' said the gardener. 'Well, to be accurate, the God you made up. The one who turned out to be just the way you expected.'

'And you?' she asked.

He gave an enigmatic smile. 'I'm the one who won't turn out to be the God you expect.'

And they walked on...

Phantom

One other thought about our muddles and mistakes.

Maurice Flitcroft was the world's worst golfer. Or so the presenter on the telly claimed. Having lost his job as a crane driver he decided to follow his dream of entering the British Open Golf Championship. Even though he'd never played a round of golf in his life. He didn't even own a set of clubs. But he went ahead and entered anyway. He got in and set a new world record. He took more shots than anyone has ever taken to get round the course. In a scene from the film that tells this tale, *The Phantom of the Open*, when Maurice meets Seve Ballesteros he tells Seve he is not nervous because he finds his mistakes are a chance to learn something new. 'Love your mistakes, Seve,' Maurice says. That's quite an attitude isn't it? Most of the time I hate my mistakes. They embarrass me. I want to get everything right. And yet... life just doesn't function like that. In his song *Anthem*, Leonard Cohen sings the lines – 'Ring the bells that still can ring, forget your perfect offering, there's a crack, a crack in everything, that's how the light gets in.' In chapter 4 of his second letter to the Simpsons, sorry I mean the Corinthians, Paul describes us all as pots with cracks in, or crackpots if you like, and God shines out through those cracks to others. I'll leave you to make the connections between Maurice, Leonard and good ol' St Paul.

Maverick

The recent movie *Top Gun: Maverick* has surprised everyone by being a whopping success, the biggest film of 2022. It's a confident, optimistic piece of escapism, the kind of film we don't make so much these days, and I figure it's that which has drawn audiences. In these tricky times people are hungry for a chance to forget for two hours and lose themselves in a vision of jets whirling and diving, and Tom Cruise steaming about on his motorbike as the bronze sun slowly sets behind him. It's a film full of attractive, intelligent, highly capable young men and women, right at the top of their game. The thing crackles and shimmers with rippling muscles and sharp one-liners. Much as I enjoyed the film it sent me racing back to a few lines in Jeremiah's biblical blog, chapter 9 verses 23–24. *Let not the strong boast in their strength, or the wise about their wisdom, or the wealthy about their riches, but let them boast that they truly know me, the living God, who is righteous and just and loving.*

For a while I saw myself as something of a failed Christian because I felt I could not reach the dizzy heights of being a

GOOD PERSON. But that experience led me to realise afresh that it's not about how great I am, but how good God is. Not what I can achieve, but how caring and compassionate he is, and the way he is willing and able to work though this bumbling bloke who keeps tripping up. And whether we have biceps or bifocals. Or both. Or neither. That's not the point. We might have an Oscar, a Nobel Prize, a first in Astro Physics, a cycling proficiency certificate, or even a Blue Peter badge. The true wonder and glory of this life is found in the way God has come close to us in Jesus, and that we can get to know him a little better each day.

What We Can

As the woman anoints him with her exorbitant perfume, he can see the disdain on the sneers of those around, their thoughts scrawled large, like newsprint, across their faces. So Jesus says, 'Don't judge her, because you don't understand, she has done a beautiful thing, she has done what she could…'

And so he looks around today. At us. This mishmash we call humanity.

And he waits to see what we will do with our time and strength, our ideas and gifts.

Still saying to those who think they know better. 'Don't judge, because you don't understand, these others have done a beautiful thing, they have done what they could… to make life better, not worse.'

And that's who we are, people who do what we can, not wasting energy on the need to judge what we don't understand, but doing what we can, with our strengths and weaknesses, our personalities and experience, our fear and courage.

We do what we can.

Mark 14 v 3–9

Amazed

It's a word that is overused today really. Amazing. Along with awesome, game-changer and legend. (And let's face it – a legend is something that is old and untrue – so, not exactly a compliment when you unpack it!) But before I stray too far into grumpy old man territory... back to amazement. Because that's how the story of the forgiven and healed paralysed man through the roof ends. With jaws dropping. Clunk! Clunk! Clunk! Amazement everywhere. People were staggered. Sidewhacked. Flummoxed. Their heads span and their hearts pumped. They probably grinned like that old Cheshire cat. Not very religious really. Not very tidy. But busting with life and reality and unrestrained laughter. They didn't need any liturgy to guide their response, it just spilled out of them.

Greener Grass (5000 Questions)

It's easy to miss the point, overlooking the goodness of God and just focussing on what we decide we should have. Especially in an age of dissatisfaction and complaining. The writer of Lamentations chapter 3 lives through a catastrophically hard time, he describes the experience as being beaten up by a bear, and so he makes a decision. He finds it hard at the moment to find God in the bigger things so he decides he will look for God's mercies in each new dawn, looking perhaps for those small things that are good, rather than the many things that are wrong. Or to put it another way, here's a snippet of a conversation between a disciple and a member of the crowd, overheard at a certain feast of bread and fish:

Right everyone, sit down, just sit down, that's it, it won't be long, the food's coming round.

Er… excuse me.

Yes?

I don't want to be in a group with this lot.

Sorry?

I wanna be over there. I prefer those people over there.

Look, forget about that for now. Something amazing is happening here.

Yea but over there they've got a bigger chunk of bread.

Believe me, whatever size of bread, you're all going to get enough – it's called a miracle.

Yea, but they've got a bigger chunk of miracle. It's not fair. And their bit of grass is greener than ours. More comfy. Look we've got some stones and dusty bits here. See?

Listen – you're focussing on the wrong thing – this is a miracle, you're going down in history.

Well could we go down in history with a bigger, neater chunk of bread please.

No! You're missing the point! You'll all end up with more than plenty.

Well what about the fish?

What about the fish?

Our bit doesn't look as nice as theirs over there.

It doesn't matter!

But suppose our miracle is smaller than theirs.

It won't be.

Well there's 52 in our group and only 48 over there. I've been counting. You said we'd all be in groups of 50.

So?

So there's more people to feed over here.

Have you seen the size of it?

The size of what?

The fish! 48 or 52 – it's not enough without the miracle.

Well they'd better not get a better miracle over there than we get over here.

Agh! A miracle's a miracle's a miracle. You're all getting the same! People will be talking about this day forever. You'll be famous!

As famous as that other lot?

What other lot?

You know that lot at the wedding in Cana, when he turned water into wine. Will we be as famous as them?

Aggghh! Just shut up and eat your bread and fish. Look, here's your bit now.

I'll never eat that much! It's way too big, have you got a smaller portion?

I'll give you more than a smaller portion in a minute...

More

And just to head off on a tangent here, Jesus did extravagant miracles involving both bread and wine – and on both occasions he gave way more than people needed. Twelve baskets of leftovers, six massive jars of the best wine. More than enough. For everyone. And then he took bread and wine and today offers it to us as the means of remembering and celebrating his life and humility and courage and love and understanding and truth and hope and empathy and sacrifice and death and resurrection. And once again there is more than enough. For everyone. This source of forgiveness and hope and new life will never run out.

Broken

The director of the series *The Chosen,* a new dramatisation of the gospels, tells of his life falling apart, just when he thought he was going to make it big. He had plans to make a big budget Christian film, and found a few financial backers, including a wrestling company and a maker of horror films. Other companies got on board too and there was a plan to make more faith-based movies. Dallas Jenkins had become a Hollywood director with a bright future. He had the finance and permission to have full creative control over the films. Then everything fell apart. The film bombed at the box office and the backers fled. Suddenly he had nothing, and no way forward. Dallas was broken and confused. Then his wife sensed a word of encouragement from God, about the feeding of the 5000 and the way God can do impossible maths. To find out more look up 'What God told me about my failure that led to The Chosen - Dallas Jenkins' on YouTube.

But the reason I mention this is often people following God find themselves in low places, in difficult times, their own plans lying like wreckage around them. Think of Mary from Nazareth, engaged to be married, planning a big village wedding, looking forward to having a family with a good husband. Everything coming together just right... till an angel showed up. And her life fell apart at the seams. How could she explain this to her fiancé Joe? To her family who would see nothing but shame in the situation? To her village who would feast on the rumours and take bets on who the father could be…

Small talk

There were all kinds of theories about who it might be, a whole ocean of stories washing up on our shore. That's why we had to hold the meeting, to give voice to the rumours, to turn the whispers to outright accusation. After all, who doesn't enjoy a tasty heft of village gossip. Especially when it's seasoned with a large dose of self-justification.

- They said it was a shepherd.

- Who did?

- 'They'.

- Yea, well I heard it was a Roman. And I heard she didn't put up a fight.

- I heard it was an angel.

- Whoever heard of an angel coming down and mixing it with a woman?

- That's blasphemy.

- Well look at the Nephilim in ancient days – weren't they from angels?

- That was back then and nothing good came of it anyway.

- I heard it was Joseph. You know, not able to contain himself.

- Well you'd know all about that.

- How dare you!!

- How dare **you**!! I'll show you 'not containing myself' in a minute when you feel the impact of my fist in your eye socket.

- Order. Order. This is getting us nowhere.

- There are other rumours.

Silence, then…

- What d'you mean?

- Well, you know, that it might all mean something.

- Ha! Of course it means something, it means a silly girl has been playing around and now there's a curse on all of us.

- We should bring her here, make her pay.

- Good luck with that, she's left town. Earlier today. Hoofed off with that fiancé of hers. Neither of them looked happy.

- Well, there you go, that proves it then. Guilty and getting out of town. That's the last we'll hear of them.

- Or the baby.

- Shame. I mean… who are we going to talk about now?

- Well her cousin's had a baby and she's way too old for that sort of thing.

- Don't tell me, I bet there was an angel involved in that as well… come on. Let's go looking for someone else we can blame about something…

- I like mysteries.

- What?

- I said I like mysteries, and maybe there's a mystery in all this. I want to find out more.

- Here's a mystery for you – why are you so bonkers? Come on…

Natural and Supernatural

Why does God work like this? Choose the most inappropriate way of bringing his son into the world? Choose a road that is messy and inappropriate and looks all wrong. Why can't it be nice and tidy and acceptable to everyone? I suppose the obvious answer is so that we rely on him. Indeed time after time in the Bible God deliberately chooses the weaker, unexpected people. Choosing the weak over the strong, the foolish over the wise. Taking ordinary folk and doing something extraordinary with and through them. But that doesn't stop it being stressful and lonely and full of questions on these roads less travelled.

So back to the Christmas story... Mary flees the village before she is starting to show. Before the rumours kick in. She hurries to see her older cousin. Another woman pregnant against the odds. And Cousin Liz gives her the best gift possible. Before Mary says a thing Liz confirms that Mary's baby is from God. She tells her the one thing she could not have known unless God was at work here. And then Mary gets some very practical help too. She stays with Liz and they talk about pregnancy and motherhood and all that goes with it. And she sees her cousin give birth. They go through the whole thing together. All of this strengthening Mary for the time when she must go back and face everyone with her startling news, now that she is clearly carrying a child inside. Spiritual and sensible help. Supernatural and natural.

Reminds me of that time Peter got busted out of prison by an angel in Acts chapter 12, verses 6–17. He is locked up and guarded by soldiers, but that's no match for an angel who can put guards to sleep and make prison gates open all on their own. When Pete rocks up on the doorstep of a prayer meeting we get one of those great comedy moments. Servant Rhoda opens the door, sees him, shrieks, slams the door again and runs back inside to tell those who are praying fervently for Peter's release that he is indeed out there. Released. Still stranded on the doorstep twiddling his thumbs and whistling a happy tune. You couldn't make it up. And then, we get the practical, sensible bit. Verse 17 tells us that he went away for a while. So having been busted out by a heavenly warrior, Peter then slips away quietly. Keeping his head down. He doesn't outright claim that if he gets arrested again he'll get angelically busted out again. He thinks on his feet and takes time out. And it seems to me that this is how God helps us. Miraculously and logically. The two working in tandem.

Part 3:
The Great Influencer

An Old Reading

There is an old reading that I have just tracked down. It took me a while but having the whole universe at my fingertips on the world-wide-webternet was a big help. It's a reading called *One Solitary Life* by James Allan Francis, and was a part of a sermon he once gave. It's about the life of Jesus, how he was born in an obscure village, the child of a peasant woman. He never wrote a book or owned a home, never went to college or did the usual things that accompany greatness. Yet no army or navy, government or king can come anywhere near matching the impact and influence this one life has had on the world. It's a remarkable poem, and one that is still being shared today. Just Google *One Solitary Life* and you should come across it.

Being an influencer is a job description these days. I used to joke about how I'd like to be paid for being a 'thinker' – you know, sitting there with my forehead pressed to my fist contemplating the wonder of all created things. And then maybe occasionally stringing a sentence together in a way that no one has ever considered before. In between cups of tea and Jaffa cakes. (And no it's not a cake, it's a biscuit.) But I digress… these days you can earn money by being an influencer, e.g. showing people how to apply their make-up, or the best ways to pack your shopping, or explaining the lifecycle of a cockroach in a 500-part series. Or anything you want really. If you can get an audience, then you can get sponsors. As long as your material is original. So here's another original thinker, another kind of influencer.

The Great Influencer

Not one who merely talks through a phone or tablet screen,

not mentioning the new and trendy products that he's been

wearing or using – not here for applause or merchandise,

but with truth on his lips and raw kindness in his eyes.

He's not sponsored to sell or say something fake,

not here to push anything, he's not on the take.

Yet he's the greatest influencer the world has ever known,

in it for the universe, and for all those lonely or alone.

He's been spotted in the places where the mud and anger fly,

in the darkness on the edge of town, where people live and die.

And most commonly he's pinned to a form of ancient death,

held there by a tyranny that stole his choking breath.

Yet from that place of dirt and darkest desecration

he emerged with wounded hands gripping seeds of resurrection.

Eternal seeds of strength, forgiveness, faith and hope and light,

right here in the midst of a world that's far from right.

He continues to walk the spattered pavements of the planet,

with eternal perspective, from the one who first began it,

Living life with open hands, and challenging the proud,

bringing comfort and strength to those lost in the crowd.

For some the merest glimpse of him changes everything,

for others it can be a more dramatic happening.

While others still cry out and long for something more,

and others wonder what their time on earth is for,

his influencing voice goes on speaking day by day,

that calm and quiet call on life's precious, wounded way.

Ordinary Things

There's a scene I love in the film *Chariots of Fire*, when Christian athlete Eric Liddell is speaking to the trackside crowd after winning a race. He talks about running and competing and placing a bet, about energy and will, and about being out of work and going home to a burnt dinner. And he relates all this to having faith, and the kingdom of God. There's an ease about the way he knits all these things together. It's not embarrassing or forced in any way. I watch that and I think about Jesus. Because it seems to me that's what he did. He took the things of ordinary life and used them to remind people of the ways of the kingdom. Stuff that they would go home and use or eat or work with. Bread, fish, farming, gardening, yeast, grapes, nets, lights, dust. And stuff that would then remind them of his stories and teaching.

I have an old Coke advert that I show sometimes. It features a young woman on a beach with a can in her hand, she is secretly admiring a man who is out in the water. When he turns and walks back to the beach he smiles at her and pulls on his shirt. She looks horrified. He's a priest! Unfazed he walks over to her, runs his thumb up the can to father a few drops of conversation, and he anoints her with the moisture on his thumb. A perfect example of what Jesus was doing in his time. Taking ordinary things and using them to bring the kingdom of God to people. Folk laugh when I show the video, who'd have thought a coke can could be used in that way? Well, Jesus for one. He was regularly taking what seemed unspiritual and transforming it. Sheep, coins, corn, yeast, fish, wine… these things became unforgettable symbols of the kingdom of God. Prostitutes, collaborators, rebels, criminals, those too lost, too ill, too unclean or too sinful to come close to God, well he came close to them. He was in the business of transfiguration. Change was in the air.

A Hillside for the World

And seeing the crowds he sat down on a hillside and began to teach them, and more and more people came to hear him. Some were looking at their mobile phones at the time and so missed every third word, which led to some misunderstanding. Others were waiting to take selfies with him, while some came and took photos of the scene – Jesus calmly sitting there against the backdrop of advertising billboards, restless traffic and a thousand gleaming city lights. So small in front of the vast sprawl of modern life. Yet eager and willing to sit with those who would come and find him. Out of time and unbothered by trends and progress and popularity. And though he had no amplification or video screen or PowerPoint presentation, yet people were able to hear and see, and those with hungry hearts found his message hitting home, bringing light into their eyes, a lift in their spirits, and strength for their tired bodies. And though he was offered big-money contracts and glamorous deals by those with grand intentions, he kept his focus on the people there. Telling stories which drew them into conversation and invited them to banter with him and ask questions and offer opinions. And so he stayed on that hillside, whatever the weather, and for as long as there were people who were searching for reality and meaning, appreciation and kindness. And though at time it cost him dearly, he never complained and he always kept his focus, listening to his heavenly father and doing his work among the people.

Luke 8 v 4–15

Tuition

Before he was a successful author Michael Morpurgo was a teacher. He chose to tell stories for the last half hour of each day as he figured there was little point trying to teach. No one in the class was concentrating so close to going home. When he ran out of his own favourite tales, and found his year six class weren't enjoying other stories, he made a life-changing decision. He started making up his own. I think he was onto something with his idea about reading stories. I remember our teacher Mr Tuck reading to us at the end of a school day when I was about eight. We remember stories. We enjoy them. We might even prefer them to straightforward tuition. In the church we overlook the power of stories, thinking that straight teaching is more effective. Preachers often draw on the instruction in Paul's letters. But Jesus used anecdotes, soundbites, adventures and twisty tales of the unexpected.

Creative, Cultural and Cryptic

Wander through chapter 1 of John's gospel and towards the end you'll bump into Nathaniel, just as he meets Jesus for the first time. Nathaniel seems a little sidewhacked by the encounter, declaring that Jesus must be the rescuer they are all waiting for, but Jesus tells him to ease off the pedal a little. He wants Nathaniel to watch and wait and then make up his mind. So he says this to him, 'Keep looking and you will see the angels of God going up and down on the son of man.' A phrase which is loaded with meaning yet shrouded in mystery. The first thing to say is that when Jesus uses the phrase 'son of man' Nathaniel won't realise he is referring to himself. Nathaniel will instead think of Daniel chapter 7, in which a mysterious figure, 'one like a son of man' descends from heaven to reign over the whole world forever. So who is that son of man?

Well, Jesus makes another Old Testament reference here. Remember a certain ladder with angels going up and down? Yep, Jacob on the run, having a vision, and realising that this vision of ladders and angels can mean only one thing – 'God is here and I didn't realise it!' (More on this later.) Another thing about this ladder is that it connects heaven and earth. So – to sum up – Jesus is saying there'll be a new ladder in town, one made of flesh and bone, and he will join heaven and earth, and signify the presence of God. And that human ladder will one day rule the nations forever. See? All Nathaniel has to do is watch and learn, and he will begin to discover who this son of man is.

And this sums up perfectly the way Jesus taught. It's creative, cultural and cryptic. It's creative because it retells older bits of the Bible in a fresh way, it's cultural because these stories are part of the people's history, everyone is waiting for the son of man to turn up. And it's cryptic. Jesus doesn't spell it out, he wants to woo Nathaniel, get him mystified, and wanting to know more. Like a good whodunit. Jesus wants him to stay till the end to find out the truth, and what it can mean for the rest of the story.

Email

I have an email reminder which appears in my inbox once a week. It reminds me to look again at the ways Jesus taught. The things he used, the style of his storytelling, the props and people he included and referenced. He was interactive, he invited conversation, he used questions, his teaching opened people up rather than shutting them down. Any response was acceptable. He wanted people to experience things, not just walk away with three bullet points. They had to join the dots, read between the lines, fill in the gaps. It wasn't about finding the right answer or spotting the right meaning. On one day the story might be about loneliness for you. On another day it might be about being honest. On another day about being rescued. He taught with open hands, rather than clenched fists.

Haggling

He retold history (the prodigal son is the account of Jacob running away, but with a different ending), he used soap opera stories (the good Samaritan is like an episode of *Casualty*), he involved children, corn and money. He frequently took stories people thought they knew and then gave them a twist. In Proverbs a wise woman throws a party with wine and good food and invites everyone to come and be changed. Jesus tells a tale of a king who throws a feast and invites people to come. But they refuse! Using ridiculous excuses. No one buys a cow or a field and only afterwards goes to look at them. Abraham haggled with God over Sodom, but he was rich, powerful, male and the father of the faith. Jesus tells his tale of a powerless widow who haggles with an unjust judge. She's poor and second-class and a

43

nobody. And yet – just like Abraham, she can wrestle with God. Tales of the unexpected.

USB

The thing about parables is that they are often not about what they are about. The lost coin is not really about a woman losing a coin. It's about God never giving up on searching us out, reaching into the dark places of our lives to rescue us. Time and time again. The beauty of this parable is that the next time you lose a coin or your glasses or your car keys or your USB stick or your phone, and you are hunting high and low for them, it might well remind you of the God who never gives up hunting high and low for us, and for the bits of our lives which go astray. The house on the rock is not really about two builders and two houses, it's about the best way to live, founded on Jesus's life and teaching. It's about the way we can build bits of our lives on iffy foundations. Away from the life-affirming ways of Jesus. And we might have the lounge and the kitchen-diner set on firm stuff, but the outside toilet and the garden shed might be about to crumble in a storm. (And I'm looking at myself here.) Jesus's parables aren't about getting into heaven, they are about life on earth.

Unlocking

If you drop in on Matthew 16 v 19, you'll find Jesus giving Peter and the disciples the keys of the kingdom. This was, I believe, a saying the rabbis used about handing their teaching to their followers and inviting them to unlock it for others. Something preachers, teachers, storytellers, dramatists, writers, artists, clowns, prophets and dancers have been doing down the ages ever since. So with that in mind, here's a re-telling of one of his stories, and perhaps it might serve as an unlocking of sorts. A family have gathered for the reading of a will...

Barn Fever

'Welcome one and all, family and er... interested parties... of Mr Richard Fool for the reading of his will, following his sad and mysterious demise after the completion of his final barn of storage for squirrelling away his obscene wealth. As you know Rich Fool was not a man who suffered er... fools gladly, and he was a man of great wealth, in land, funds and er... barns. He had a lot of barns. More than he needed, it turned out. He spent so much time and energy building his barns he ran out of time for living or enjoying time with others. I believe he had no real friends or acquaintances, as he spent much of the time talking to himself, which is what brought him to the conclusion he needed to build an estate full of barns. Barns, barns, barns. Barns everywhere. He'd had a ferociously good crop that year and sadly this only led to him worrying about losing it all. I heard it said that, as he watched his workers gather the massive harvest in, he mumbled to himself, 'If this lot gets eaten by mice it'll be the worst year ever.' I'm not sure that even the Pied Piper could have rustled up enough rodents to munch their way through even a fraction of that bumper crop. Rich Fool was a man who had been blessed with so much, and it's clear to so many of us that he had shedloads to share, sadly it just wasn't clear to him. Anyway, on with the will, are you sitting comfortably? Well, you don't need to, because it's shockingly short and sweet. 'I leave everything,' he says 'to... me! Me me me. Yes,' he says, 'it's all mine. All mine

mine mine.' And that's it, somehow the old fool thought he could take the lot with him, so it looks like the mice will be fed well for the next couple of decades. I think there are a few barns going spare though if anyone would like to inherit a few of those?'

Luke 12

Three Stories

And continuing on this theme of unlocking the nature of the kingdom, here are three stories of my own. No clues. Just read them, think on them, and react to them. There are no right or wrong answers. Any response is fine. I've left a bunch of blank pages after them for anything you might like to scribble, about the stories or any other bits of this book. If you need more space to react you could always grab a notepad/journal/parchment/iPad/stone tablet.

The Walls

The walls had risen around them, so slowly they had not noticed. But now they felt it, the bricks of cynicism and lost identity and blame. And of drifting in a world cut loose from its moorings. And so they gathered to discuss a way out. Some offered trinkets and magic, some suggested they push against the walls with everything they could muster. A few spoke of the invisible God. But this raised questions of responsibility and relationship. Precious gems and symbols, mustered strength and inner ability did not call for future commitment. Plus they might be making fools of themselves. But the few continued with their requests. To go further than their own ideas and to take a step of simple yet profound trust. To call out to the invisible God and to see where there might be a way out. So they did. And there was no spectacular moment, the walls did not crumble or explode. The sun did not suddenly rise on a new dawn. The bricks remained. Yet some felt as if their eyes were open in a new way. Some felt very little. Some were hopeful for the first time in years. And little by little the bricks crumbled, or some of the group found the strength to remove them. And some of the bricks remained but looked different now. The walls went on. But for some they had lost their power.

The Treasure Chest

Two friends, a man and a woman, were walking across a field when they came across an old wooden box sticking out of the ground. There was a note attached to it, telling them that if they looked inside they would find some precious things. So they pulled the chest out of the ground and opened the lid. They immediately shut it again. The smell was terrible! When they eventually had another look, their hands over their noses, they saw that the chest was full of old bits of junk and rubbish, covered in cobwebs and rust and grease and dirt. They wondered what to do, could the note about the precious things just be made up? They thought about just leaving the box and walking away. But little by little they took out the bits and pieces of rubbish. It took a while, but eventually, down at the bottom, underneath everything else, they spotted something sparkling amongst the cobwebs and dust. They reached inside, their hands now covered in grease and dirt, and lifted a handful of tiny precious stones. They were rich.

Lonely Giant

There was once a tall, lonely giant. He often went to social events but everyone else was so much smaller, so it was difficult to make eye contact or conversation. And therefore difficult to make friends. Eventually he stopped going and just hid, hunched in his cave. Weeks went by, and he started running out of food, so, feeling worse than ever he snuck out of his cave as it was growing dark and slipped down to the local shop. He had to stoop to walk in, of course he did, everywhere was the wrong height for him, and he had to crouch very low to reach the shelves. But eventually he filled his basket with a few bits of food, and a rope and he hurried to the counter. 'Can you reach that can for me please?' said a voice. He looked around but couldn't see anyone. 'I'm down here,' said the voice. He looked down. There was a small person. A very small person. She smiled at him. 'I can't reach the top shelves,' she said, 'and I need a can of beans.' He reached up and took the can of beans and handed them down. 'Funny isn't it?' she said as they left the shop together. 'What is?' he said. 'You being so big,' she said, 'me being so small. I wish I was tall like you.' 'No you don't' he said. 'Yes, I do. Life would be a lot easier.' 'I wish I was small like you,' said the giant, and there was a tear in his eye. 'I feel a fool,' he said, 'like I always stick out and am never much use.' 'You got me a can of beans today,' she said, 'that's really good. You've got some bread there, why don't I make us beans on toast.' Later she asked him, 'Why did you buy the rope?' as she cooked the beans on her small stove. He didn't answer so she nodded and frowned. 'Don't get rid of yourself,' she said. 'You're too important. If nothing else we can go shopping together and I can get the low stuff and you can reach the top shelves. Better that way.' And so he went home, sat hunched in his cave, and thought about feeling lonely, and going shopping with a small person who needed his help.

Startling

One more sideways take on an unexpected biblical adventure, this one inspired by my good friend Steve. As I mentioned at the start of this book, it's easy to forget the startling, mind-bending nature of the life of Jesus, so here's a different take on the lesser-known story of the widow of Nain.

Private Investigations

He sees himself as the local private eye, the qualified crime buster in cases like these. Not that he has any qualifications, just a keen eye and a nose for a good mystery. Most of the witnesses are still in shock. They can barely string a sentence together. The official in charge didn't see what happened, too busy looking the wrong way. He just heard the gasps and the cry. Only one thing for it. Call in the mother.

'So,' he says, indicating she take a seat, 'this happened around what time?'

The woman's make-up is smudged, her cheeks flushed. She sniffs.

'About midday,' she says, 'we were all out in the street.'

'In public eh? A crime hidden in plain sight then.'

'Oh I'd hardly call it that.'

'You leave the calling of it to me, Mrs Smith. I'm the one who knows round here. Go on.'

'Well, a stranger appeared from nowhere. Watched us pass by and then...' she gasps for a moment and catches her breath.

'Take your time Mrs Smith, this catastrophe has clearly had a traumatic affect.'

'Oh I'd hardly say that.'

'You leave the saying to me Mrs Smith. I'm the one who knows round here. Go on.'

'Well, it was startling, the way he approached us with such confidence. He just walked right up. I've never seen anything like it. We didn't know what he was going to do. Why he was even here. It was really unsettling. We just froze.'

'Clearly. Such a dastardly deed is unimaginable.'

'Oh I'd hardly describe it like that.'

'You leave the describing to me, Mrs Smith. I'm the one who knows round here. Go on.'

'Well it all happened so quickly. He leaned over, stretched out his hand, said something and it was done.'

'Dear dear. Oh dear dear. You have my sympathies. This is terrible.'

'Terrible? Hardly!'

'Mrs Smith, of course it's terrible. There's a dead body in a coffin here, and a dangerous stranger on the loose...'

'No there isn't. There's an empty coffin, and my dead son alive and well, and scoffing fish and fig pie with the stranger who invaded his funeral and resurrected him.'

'What!?'

'You may not know as much as you think. This is the best day of our lives. Investigate that Mr Private Eye!'

Luke 7 v 11–17

Beginning Again

Just as an aside here, this woman being a widow, she had already lost her husband, and in losing her son she had lost all the men in her life. In that culture it left her in a perilous situation, with little means of earning an income. So Jesus not only resurrects her son, but he also resurrects her. Her life can begin again.

Part 4:
With Us

God is With

Take time to stroll through chapter 5 of Matthew's gospel and chapter 6 of Luke's account, and you'll stumble across Jesus telling everyone this, you could say it was his mission statement:

'God is with the poor and those who know they need God,

God is with the gentle and humble ones,

With those who are hungry and thirsty for what is right,

Those who love peace and mercy.

God is with those whose hearts are broken,

Those who do not have enough,

Those who are pushed down, insulted, and damaged by others.'

And then he demonstrated this, by living it out for three years.

Huge Handfuls

And in his living he brought laughter, comfort, full life, kindness, and the kingdom of God, and he brought these things in great measure, huge handfuls of the stuff. At times people didn't know what had hit them. They wondered and questioned and chased after him. And those who were second-class citizens, the women and children, and those who were sick and poor, didn't stay away. They sensed change and respect, they sensed mercy and dignity. They felt wooed by Jesus, never shunned or judged by him. No cold shoulder here. And when he told stories it created conversation, Jesus wanted to know what they thought, what they heard, where they saw themselves in his stories. These things created relationship. And to him that was way better than spirituality or religion.

Awareness

There is a much-misquoted verse in Habakkuk 2 verse 14. It goes like this – 'the earth will be filled with the glory of God as the waters cover the sea'. But in reality the verse reads – 'the earth will be filled with the *awareness* of the glory of God as the waters cover the sea'. It seems to me that the earth is already filled with the glory of God in so many ways. The problem is our eyes aren't always open to it, our minds aren't necessarily tuned in, and our hearts misinterpret it. We are not *aware* of it. I'll give you a brief example from a book I read recently, *The Salt Path* by Raynor Winn. It's a great read and an extraordinary true story of living against the odds. A couple in their 60s lose everything and decide to walk the South West coast path, wild camping along the way. They are short on money and the husband is unwell, but they battle on and win through. Early in the trip Raynor wanders into a churchyard and a peace descends on her there. She is quick to say that it's not a spiritual peace but a human one. And of course she may well be right. But I read her words and couldn't help wondering. She was, after all in a place which had been prayed in for centuries, a place where people had experienced the presence of God and worshipped their creator countless times. Is it so unfair to suggest she was actually experiencing something of the presence of God, something of the glory of God? But was perhaps unaware of that?

No Place

If we wander into Genesis 28 we bump into a prodigal. His name is Jacob and he's fleeing from his family, with his heart in turmoil about the way he had cheated his brother and his father before hitting the road. He falls down to sleep, perhaps with his head on his backpack, and he dreams of angels. And a stairway. With God at the top of it. When he wakes up something strikes him. No, it's not a rock hurled by his angry brother. It's the awareness of the glory of God. 'Surely God was here all the time, and I never knew it!' he exclaims. This is a particularly startling revelation for him as he is of the worldview that God doesn't travel much and is still back at home with his family. And he is running away from all that. Plus he's a cheat. So surely God would give up on him. Abandon him. But no. To misquote Psalm 139 – 'Where can I go to escape your presence? I could scurry to the ends of the earth, and you'd still be there. I could run from my family and you would not give up on me. No corner is too dark, no cave too draughty, no place too deathly or desolate for you. The night shines as bright as day to you.' God is not afraid of the dark, within us, or without. There's an old Groucho Marx joke that goes – 'Outside of a dog a book is a man's best friend, inside of a dog it's too dark to read anyway.' Well, nowhere is too dark for God. Outside or inside of anything.

Sulky

Jonah got on a pea-green boat and sailed away for a month and a day (I'm guessing about that bit) because he didn't want to take God's love to Nineveh. But that was no good, God was ahead of him, and the pagan sailors on the pea-green boat got converted in a storm. (We've stumbled into the book of Jonah now.) And as Jonah sat hunched on a half-digested seagull and half-repented in a cloud of pungent stomach gas, (notice he doesn't actually say sorry for running away) God was right there with him. And when Jonah eventually touched down in Nineveh he found God already there too. And when he lost his rag and went into a sulk about God loving people that he hated, God was there too. And when he skulked up a hillside still hoping that the Ninevites would be toasted, God was still there, waiting to ask Jonah about his anger. Jonah's anger hadn't gone anywhere, you see, it was still inside of him, festering away on why God wouldn't be the God Jonah wanted him to be.

And when Jonah shut down and wouldn't tell God why he was angry with him, God was there too, sending him a nice, cheery, sun-shading plant. Which soon became a withered, conversation-starting ex-plant. Was Jonah angry about the ex-plant? You bet he was, and it caused him to splurt out his anger and disappointment. Which gave God a chance to suggest he had every right to care about people he had made.

It could be said that the fish in Jonah is a red herring. You might have thought it was a whale, but no, it's a red herring. What truly matters is God's closing question – '…Nineveh has more than 120,000 people living in spiritual darkness, not to mention all the animals. Shouldn't I feel sorry for such a great city?'

To put it another way and to draw on the kind of question Jesus will ask much later on… Which is easier? For God to forgive and help those we hate and fear, or for a fish to swallow a man?

Misdeeds

Floods have been on the rise again in previous years. And we may sometimes find ourselves calling out for help when the weather seems to turn on us. I ran to Psalm 46 and held on with all my might, when storm Eunice came upon us, and we took a frightening pounding. *God is our refuge and strength a very present help in times of trouble.* Had the psalm been around in Noah's day it's one he might have grabbed hold of as the rains began falling. Much is debated about the nature and reality of the flood, but again this misses the point. The point that God is present in a damaged world of turmoil, the point that God is present when we feel out of control, the point that God is present when we are asked to take on difficult tasks, the point that God is present though we may not understand what is going on. We can get sidetracked by the hows and whys of the rising water and miss absorbing the real lessons here. Once again, it could be said that the flood is a red herring. Or perhaps a damp squib. Or a soggy bottom. If you see what I mean. And who knows – perhaps the flood itself was caused by a fracture in the climate, due to the destructive and wasteful lifestyles of the people of Noah's day.

In his insightful book *What is the Bible*, Rob Bell points out that many cultures had flood stories, and they usually ended with people being wiped out and the gods sitting back and rubbing their hands with glee. But not here. (Rob's book is full of great insights about various difficult Bible stories.) In the biblical account there's a rainbow and the promise that God will not choose that way again. From now on there will be another way to deal with our misdeeds, mistakes, and misdemeanours. Another way to deal with the wrong in the world. Another kind of life we can choose. As Noah disembarks from the ark God is waiting for him with a promise on his lips and a rainbow in his hand.

And with that difficult Bible passage in mind, another Jesus-shaped question… Which is easier? For God to promise us a hope and a future in which he cares for us, or for the world to be flooded?

Flashy

Wander back a few fistfuls of chapters to Genesis 37 and you'll find a flashy-coated Joe bragging to his brothers about how great he's gonna be, and how many followers he'll have. Not on Instagram. In real life. But not before he lands up in a dry well, then in slavery and then in prison. Endless days and nights of wondering and frustration and suffering and generally questioning what on earth was going on. He'd dreamt about stars bowing down to him for heaven's sake. Now he was staring through bars every day. But God was with him in every part of the journey, and Joe grew more mature with each catastrophe. He didn't realise it but he was in training. Albeit for years and years and years. Eventually he'd be running the superpower of his day.

Moses had a similar experience, he lost his privileged life in the royal family, fled from a murder scene, fed sheep for 40 years, and thought it was all over. Bring on the Horlicks and slippers. But no, God was right there with him and he'd been in training too. Life in the royal court, and long days in the desert, put him in perfect shape to haggle with Pharaoh and lead the Israelites from Egyptian slavery to Red Sea crossing freedom.

Promises

And when Simon-*I-promise-I'll-never-give-up-on-you*-Peter gave up on Jesus and fled in tears, God was with him every step of the way. (It's worth noting that it wasn't only Peter who said he'd never deny Jesus, all the other disciples said the same. Matthew assures us of this in chapter 26 of his book.)

In fact Jesus had foreseen the whole bucket of trouble, and even said to Peter beforehand, 'Afterwards, this is what I want you to do.' In other words, after the mess-up, after the big mistake, after the confusion and terror, after the tears and running and hiding and beating-yourself-up... ...this is the new future I have for you. The next step. And on the shore, while cooking a post-resurrection breakfast for the lads, and then taking them for a forgiving stroll together, Jesus doesn't ask Peter to promise he will never deny him again. He knows what Peter is like. He knows what Martha is like too. And Esther. And Ruth. And Moses. He knows us. He's the one who makes the promises. 'I won't abandon you,' he says, 'I won't leave you alone, like widows and orphans.'

Bitter

Naomi felt so desolate she changed her name to Bitter, declaring to anyone that would listen that God had left her with nothing. Absolutely nothing. Really? Strange then that her daughter-in-law Ruth was standing right next to her, having declared she would stick with Bitter no matter what came their way. Even if they both died together. This is one of the most powerful examples of God present through the hands and feet and love of another. (We've limped into Ruth chapter 1 now, by the way.) Ruth's promise is one of the most extraordinary in the Bible, the most dedicated, the most courageous. And it would change both their lives. Her broken mother-in-law would begin to repair as Ruth lays her life on the line. And as they start to work together the future would open up. Not just for Ruth and Naomi, but for the future King David and for a carpenter called Jesus. And for you and me.

In Death

And in those dark hours of John 19 vv 26–27, as Jesus looked down from that brutal cross, pinned there and being slowly murdered, he saw his mother who must have been having a terrible breakdown. So he asked John to take her home and look after her. She must have been inconsolably broken by the sight of her innocent, dearly loved son dying in such public torment. But Jesus would be with his mother even as he was confronting his own death, through the hands and feet and comfort of his best friend John.

Right There

And as I've already mentioned, a younger version of Mary, invisibly pregnant, and wondering how on earth she would tell her family and fiancé about it, fled to her cousin's only to discover God was right there on the doorstep. Waiting for her. The welcoming father watching for the arrival of this prodigal daughter. Ready with open arms in the shape of the warm and smiling Elizabeth. With the perfect greeting and the words to help her lift her heart and head once more. When my wife was pregnant for the second time and we lost the baby at eleven weeks, a nurse sat on the side of the hospital bed and gently assured us that God was with us in that experience, right there in our pain and tears and loss. I will never forget that. Her courage in doing that. Her presence and understanding representing God's presence and understanding.

Food and Music

My favourite band are known in some circles as *The only band that matters*. I wonder if you have favourite music, songs, composers, groups, genres, singers or bands? Music is a kind of universal language. From a very early age we sing and dance (more on children in part 6).

Music is a great gift to the world. It lifts us, soothes us, energises us; expresses joy and pain and doubt and longing and wonder and celebration. And worship. Worship to the God that matters. We all worship lots of other small gods in life. The gods of greed, work, lust, possessions, selfishness, aggression, etc. We all do it, don't we. I do anyway. And those gods sap the life from us, suck the energy, drain the joy and compassion. Make us less satisfied. A lot of advertising is based on these gods. Feeding on the idea that the vacuum inside can be filled with more stuff. More stuff that can only make the vacuum bigger. Which means the advertisers can then sell us more stuff to fuel the fires of dissatisfaction. (I can speak with some authority on this – I get suckered by advertising all the time!)

And then there is the God that matters. The one who understands why we take diversions down the dirt tracks of these other gods. The God who knows why it's so tempting to slip away once more and return to the pigsty of the prodigal. The God who cares about our lust, greed, dissatisfaction and selfishness. The God who offers another kind of food and drink, the kind that is free. And won't chip away at our precious humanity. And in the words of Isaiah and his song number 55, the kind of nourishment that is sustaining and life-giving and satisfying and reliable and refreshing and produces a healthy harvest. Food and drink from a God whose thinking and imagination and ways of living are far bigger, far higher than ours. The food and drink that nourished Jesus regularly. 'I have food you know nothing about,' he said once when his friends were fretting about bread. And he frequently slipped away to reconnect with the only God that matters. Frequently spotted what his heavenly father was doing and joined in.

The God that matters believes in resurrection and believes in us. And he understands how hard and disappointing this life can be. The God that matters has walked its uneven paths, experienced the lonely nights and the days of distrust and danger and frustration. The God that matters knows what he's talking about. And he invites us into the conversation, invites us into the journey of a lifetime, to walk with him and little by little by little to get to know him better. To have good days and bad days with that, sometimes veering off the path or tripping over our feet, but always invited to keep going and learning. Often from making our mistakes. To feed on his living bread and to drink that living water, which often unknowingly bubbles out of us towards others. The water that is, not the bread, hard to imagine bread bubbling out. But I'm sure we may well leave trails of crumbs unknowingly too.

(It's The Clash by the way. In case you were wondering. My favourite group who broke up long ago and at some point acquired the tagine *The only band that matters.*)

(Oh and I must confess to pinching the phrase *The only God that matters* from Rob Bell, it was his use of this phrase that made me think of The Clash, and *The only band…* etc.)

Part 5:

Dull Days and Full Days

Parties and Prayer Meetings

One of the surprising things about Jesus is this – he got into trouble for enjoying himself. Turning parties into prayer meetings and prayer meetings into parties. On one occasion a despised and hated tax collector climbed a tree and found more than leaves and twigs. He got an audience with a religious celebrity who then came to his house for a slap-up meal. And when the tax collector got converted he started giving away free money. No doubt the whole town lived it up a little. Not your average religious conversion story, is it?

Jesus attended at least three funerals and disrupted all of them with a little thing called resurrection. At one of them he hadn't even been invited. He just spotted a body in a casket. Mourners would have been hired, and at least one heart was in a million pieces, yet Jesus didn't even stop to inquire the young corpse's name. He just slipped past the pall bearers and woke the guy up. No doubt mourning turned to... well... screams, laughter, cheers, gasps, and dancing. Probably a whole mix of that lot. When Jesus spotted another tax collector (he was fond of those misfits) he invited him to follow him, and that all ended up at a party. With lots of other tax collectors. And other outcasts too. No wonder the religious elite accused Jesus of mixing it with scum – they weren't insightful enough to see what was really going on. God was in town. And that meant the out-crowd were fast becoming the in-crowd. The discarded were being rescued. The mistreated and manhandled were being valued and respected.

Religious Rules

He just wouldn't stick within the strict religious lines. He wouldn't separate life into neat boxes. If he were around today he'd be accused of mixing religion with politics. And religion with education. And religion with sex. And religion with pleasure. And religion with happiness. And religion with the tough questions. You name it he'd mix it. He just wouldn't be predictable. Plus his edge-of-the-seat tales were not nice clean Christian testimonies. His funny stories were not cheesy sermon starters. They featured passion and violence, shocking humour and dysfunctional families, reckless managers and wasteful farmers. I wonder whether he'd be accepted by a Christian publisher these days. He might well have to censor some of his work. But Jesus refused to stay out of any parts of life. He wanted access. To the real bits. And he came at the far-flung corners of reality with a smile and a mouthful of witty dialogue. He'd come to bring us life, and that meant behaving badly at times. At least according to the social standards of his day.

Lines

In his book *What is the Bible* Rob Bell points out that the Sidonians were a cursed nation. Sidon was Noah's great grandson, cursed through the line of Ham and his son Canaan. Years later, according to Judges 10, they oppressed Israel for a while. The prophets were not impressed and Isaiah, Jeremiah, Ezekiel, Joel and Zechariah all got in on the act, pronouncing judgment and retribution on 'those people'.

66

But Jesus clearly never got the memo, because he went around happily healing and blessing them. He visited the place a few times, and even compared them favourably with Israel, using them as a yardstick to measure the lack of response in towns such as Bethsaida and Korazin.

Nip over to Luke 4 v 26 and you find yourself in Nazareth, where Jesus is enthusiastically telling the tale of Elijah being sent to help the widow of Zarephath in – guess where – yes, Sidon. I can imagine him now, smiling as he talked of it. You can't see smiles on the faces of the crowd though. They didn't politely say, 'This is the word of the Lord' after he'd finished. No, they tried to bump him off, attempting to hurl him over a cliff edge for that serious misdemeanour. Folks wanted him to take the sides they were taking, to dislike those they disliked. Draw the lines in the sand that they were drawing. But he was having none of it. Bear this in mind when you read of a Roman centurion having his servant healed in Matthew 8. I mean, what have the Romans ever done for us?

No Guru

The heartening, unique thing about Jesus is that he is not only our example and inspiration, but the source of our strength and abilities. If we saunter for a moment over to the first chapter of a letter to a ragtag bunch known as the Colossians, in verses 16 and 17 we discover the jaw dropping assurance that everything was made through him, and he holds everything together. He's not merely a wise teacher, or a guru, or a life-coach. Not merely a shoulder to cry on, and way more than a pick-me-up after a rough night. He is the one we look to for opportunities, for the right words to say, for the appropriate action to take, for the best timing of events etc. It's not only about our strength, but his, it's not only about our intellect, but his. And with him we may often find ourselves nudged towards things which expose our own weakness. So we are compelled to lift our heads and yell, 'Help!'

There is a supernatural side to following Jesus. It can be tempting to be a little humanist about this man from Nazareth, as if he calls us and so we must 'do our best' to follow him. But I don't buy that. I'm scuppered if it's all about me! Thankfully it's not. He is our example and enabler. Our song and our strength. The road and the fuel. The reason and the resource. As an old saying goes, when God calls he also provides.

W

And perhaps we should consider that W word here. Weakness. Paul writes about God's power being made perfect in our weakness. Not just managing with it, not just getting by, not just putting up with it, but the two working together. His power and our weakness make the perfect combination at times. It's not that we should get better at being Christians and therefore won't need God. The perfect way is that we are weak and need God's power.

I also think God loves to use us in his world, each of us a vital part, a vital sign of his presence in the universe. Not as a last resort but as a first resort. We may think of God as a means to an end, asking him to do things for us, but it seems to me we are called to be co-workers, co-creators, co-investors in life with him. I think he takes a shedload of pleasure from involving us in caring for others, in creating things and ideas and possibilities, in guiding others, in being signs of hope, in teaching others, in listening to others, in enabling others to value and enjoy life. Maybe that's why God is invisible, so we can put skin in the game.

More Alive

It may well be that Jesus's stories, encounters, sayings, relationships, conversations were intended to show us more of life. Helping us to be more connected to life and what makes it worth living. Don't get me wrong, I'm not saying Jesus makes life easier, or more exciting, or a non-stop party. Most Christians in the world are poor, marginalised, powerless, and struggling. And Jesus came from a poor background himself. He knew all about real life in a tough climate. 'In this world you'll have trouble,' he told us. But he was 100% tuned into the world and what made it turn. Totally focussed on what made life worth living. He also knows what it is to live through times when not much happens. When we are waiting for the extraordinary to kick in, desperate for some change and improvement.

His life was very ordinary indeed for three decades. We have little idea what he got up to between returning from Egypt as a young boy and getting baptised at 30. We do know he had a blast in a certain temple visit at the age of 12. Stroll over to Luke 2 v 41–52 and you can join the crowd that a young Jesus is holding in the palm of his hand. This trip may well have been like going to Disneyland or Thorpe Park for us today. A world full of adventure and promise for him. The temple! The place where folk believed that the living God lived. Jesus got so absorbed in the trip that he stayed behind when everyone else went home. He must have found a bed with one of the priests or scribes or Pharisees, first-century Airbnb maybe? Because he was there for at least three days. I reckon his mum and dad must have grounded him for the next 18 years. That's why we don't have much action for a while.

Jesus on a Dull Day

Jesus on a dull day,
There were many of these,
When nothing much came his way,
Just hammers, nails and bits of trees.

He's famous for the full days,
Of miracles and signs,
Of arguments with Pharisees
And weddings full of wine.

But Jesus had the dull days,
With not much going on,
So he understands our own ways,
When the streams of life meander on.

And Jesus had his bad days,
When the world it brought him low,
When friends and enemies alike
Just did not want to know.

Being fully human, now that meant
Living life like us,
Knowing arguments and banter,
Frustrations, fears, frowns and fuss.

And taking all that with him,
Washing feet on his knees,
He went from Gethsemane to Calvary,
To hammers, nails and killing trees.

Jesus had his dull days,
Thirty years and more,
God with skin on, full of life,
That's what he came here for.

Two Mums

Two mothers, two sisters, couldn't always steer Jesus the way they wanted him to go. They had their ideas, their plans for their sons, but their view was limited, they could only look through a glass darkly, through a smudged and dusty window. If we gate-crash a wedding in Cana in John 2, we find a mother urging her boy to get going. She had birthed him, nursed him, soothed his scrapes and bruises, fed him, and carried him through the night to safety in Egypt. She knew her son better than anyone. So here she is, her hand squeezing his shoulder. *You can do something, so get going, get involved, son.* How many times before had she said that, tried to force his hand, nudge his elbow a little. Would it be this time? Would the new wine finally start flowing?

Later, as we stand on the edge of a large crowd in Mark 3 v 21, we may spot her urging him to calm down, worried that there is too much wine flowing now, too much expectation on him. *Come home son, be safe, this road's starting to look rocky. You look as if you're losing it a bit.* But no. He must walk on, and risk her misunderstanding. And here's her sister now, Salome, kneeling in the dust of Matthew 20, with her vision of the way things should be. Her head full of a future Prime Minister needing righthand men. *When you're powerful and in control, make my boys powerful too. Please give them importance and influence.* They will have influence, but not the way she imagines. These two sisters, sometimes right, sometimes mistaken, will one day glimpse the best morning ever. All their hopes and plans seen differently then, in the light of the new dawn, and the rising of the son.

Life

I reckon that when Jesus spoke of bringing life in its fullness, he meant something about another kind of reality. One not offered on our screens or billboards or internet ads. One in life's gaps, the God of small miracles. The God of the smile, and the new dawn, the God who believes forgiveness is way better than finding fault, the God of the brighter truth, the God of impossible odds. This seems to me to be the problem with the atheist worldview. It makes everything somehow a bit less, a tad smaller, reduces the colour a little, removes a dimension. It robs us of the possibility of things we can only do, see, discover, experience, share when God slips alongside us in the guise of a traveller on a road, the God who opens up his living word to us and brings eternity into our often-mundane reality.

For example the Bible says we're made a little lower than the angels (Psalm 8 v 5) and made in the image of God (Geneses 1 v 26). To say we are just another animal robs us of that great privilege, identity and honour. God has put eternity in our hearts, the writer of Ecclesiastes tells us. Let's not lose that. The beauty of those moments when the creator whispers to us in the pause of a typical day; or smiles on us through the clouds on an atypical day. Folks often talk today of things the universe is offering them, well let's think bigger, let's raise the stakes, let's look to the one who *made* the universe, and what he is offering us. The one who invented colour, the one who thought of a baby's gurgle, the one who finetuned uncontrollable laughter, and imagined an endless supply of tunes that 12 notes might conjure. The one who pictured a caterpillar turning into liquid in its cocoon then reforming into a butterfly with 600 scales in every square millimetre on its wings. All perfectly formed and arranged in the right, stunning pattern. Every time. And having imagined all that, he set them loose in the world. Yes. Really.

Image

That said I do appreciate that it's not necessarily easy to believe in a good and kind God, especially if we have been hurt by others. We all wear the image of God, and when we disappoint, disrespect or damage others it can seem to them as if God is like that. Likewise, in those moments when we are kind, patient, courageous, selfless, and understanding, we are communicating something to others about the goodness of God. I often think the sight of a parent being caring towards their child is one of the greatest sermons.

'As a parent is kind, forgiving and understanding to their children so God is tender and compassionate to us.' That's my retelling of Psalm 103 verse 11. Likewise one person looking out for another, a stranger helping a friend, one person listening to another, someone offering a kind word. All of these are living sermons, signs of God's love present in the world. To loosely quote the Christian runner, Eric Liddell, 'Everything we do has the potential to draw people closer to God or drive them a little further away.' We all have the superpower of a smile and a caring attitude, and as we are the image of God, so our very being can speak of his presence.

The Weather

Trusting in God can be both a simple and complex thing. I can believe that God cares deeply about me, and that he is bigger than all my troubles and able to help me and provide all I need. I can believe that he knows and understands me better than anyone. And yet AT THE SAME TIME, I can worry about the weather, the future, my work, my home, my family, money, crime, rats, getting older, upsetting people, this book, that conversation I just had, and my immense ability to say the wrong thing in the wrong way. These things can all be happening alongside each other. Adult worries and childlike faith. Running in tandem inside my being. And I doubt if I'm very different from other folk on this issue.

A Few Glimpses of Full Life...

...and some YouTube clips if you want to glimpse them for yourself.

There is a 7-minute YouTube clip of Billy Joel and his band performing one of his epic songs called *Scenes from an Italian Restaurant (live from Long Island)*. Watch the saxophonist, the guy not only plays two instruments at various times, he acts out some of the scenes from the song, and also sings and plays air guitar every so often. Oh and he leaps about a lot and looks like he's having the greatest of times. And then there's Billy himself, pummelling the piano like Jerry Lee Lewis, and pounding the floor with his white sneakers. Whenever I watch it I feel just that little bit more alive. The energy. The music. The uplifting exuberance of it all.

Charlotte Green once delivered a news item about the first ever sound recording. It featured a song, but the number wasn't exactly what you'd call catchy, and doesn't sound anything like Billy Joel in Long Island. The recording was so unusual it set Charlotte Green doing something you're not supposed to do when reading the news. Look it up for yourself on YouTube – *Radio 4's Charlotte Green cracks up on air* – it's a minute of wondrous bliss, and I challenge you to make it through without laughing yourself. Charlotte's mirth is made all the more infectious because she's not supposed to be doing it and so is doing her best to hold it in. A bit like laughing in a library, or a church service at the wrong moment. Or even perhaps at a time when Jesus good-naturedly ribs the serious-minded religious elite, who think they know all about God.

My favourite judge on the programme *The Great Pottery Throw Down* is a lovely guy called Keith. When he sees a piece of work that someone has put their heart and soul into he does something quite profound. He struggles to speak – because he's trying to hold back the tears. Keith cries at the gift of these wondrous bits of work. You can see him on YouTube if you search for this - *Every time Keith Brymer-Jones cries on the Great Pottery Throwdown*.

My wife was recently in a coffee shop when she noticed that on the table nearby a young 4-year-old girl was helping her mother because her mum had both hands bandaged. The little girl did all she could to help with various tasks. The thing is, when my wife told me about it later she was moved to tears, and I'm moved again myself as I type this now.

And one other glimpse – a friend recently described a moment in a book about the band U2, when another rock star asked the lead singer Bono why their song *One* made him cry. The lovely thing was – my friend was moved as he told us about this. And that impacted me.

And as I have been typing this, two things have happened. Last week we were with some friends in a park near our church, and one of them was carving small wooden crosses that he gives away. As he was doing this the one he was sanding broke in his fingers and I asked him about it. Well, now my wife has just come in and told me that our friend has glued the two bits together and oiled it and he wants me to have it, because he thinks it will be perfect for me. And it will be. And I feel suddenly valued and appreciated and understood a little. And then our younger daughter brought in some tiny new pumpkin-shaped lights which she is excited to hang up. So we put them up in our kitchen, a small string of ten tiny lights, and they glow and now the room looks different.

Glimpses of life. Music. Laughter. Crying. The unexpected. Creativity. Leaping about. Saxophones. Energy. Improvising. Pottery. Radio. Songs and stories that move us to tears. Friends. Repaired crosses. Sanding and carving. Pumpkins and lights. And excitement. And a million other small things. Glimpses of life. You can't explain them really. They just happen. Thank God. And I mean that in the best possible way.

Moments

These little things, that one day we will see as great,

These moments, these unexpected, unrehearsed gifts,

That smile, that listening ear, that laughter,

And those tears shared,

That communion of two lives,

Pausing to bring the kingdom come,

That dimension of heaven that breaks in when we care,

In the vital spaces between us.

When we set aside the distractions for a time,

When we see each other a little more clearly,

And appreciate the precious present, this gap in time,

The gift of now.

Part 6:
Kids and Curiosity

Comics and War Heroes

Two dustbins stand in the middle of the lane. A low rumble announces the arrival of a wooden tank, just turning the corner. There is the sound of squeaking wheels as it draws ever closer. The road is empty, quiet apart from this. The tank rumbles on, heading straight for the bins. It is well able to send them tumbling over. Then suddenly, at the last minute, the lids fly off the bins, and two figures emerge, walking sticks in hand, stabbing them straight towards the exposed driver of the tank. The tank veers of the road. A swarm of boys emerge from the roadside ditches and collide in its wake. Chasing after each other in a scramble of bodies, noise and energy.

This is not the start of *The Otterbury Incident*. But if I made it into a film it might well be. It's a book I have loved for five decades now. It's my go-to favourite kid's book. A tale of derring-do about two gangs of boys who play-act war games with sticky bombs and a wooden tank, only to find themselves embroiled in a real adventure when they come up against a bunch of ne-er-do-wells. One of them with the brilliantly threatening name of Johnny Sharp. I have loved it for most of my life and I'm sure I'll love it forever.

I guess I wanted to be part of those gangs when I was eight, and in some ways I still want to be part of them now. The chance to mess about together. To be a part of something which isn't highly organised and aiming for some kind of productive end. I recently came home to see my daughter had been chalking on our front steps. Adults don't tend to do that. Sit round on the pavement idly doodling. Takes me back to the days when we used to abandon our bikes and loll about in the gutters, daydreaming, studying insects and bantering about our comics and games and war movies. Life was an adventure back then. Now it often feels like a job to be done. A problem to be solved.

Creaky

I recently looked at a list of songs by Billy Eilish and didn't recognise any of them. My daughter Lucy, who is currently nine, did know them. When I complained about my ignorance she said, 'Welcome to the next generation, dad.' I felt old and creaky. I grew up listening to Radio One and it breaks my heart a little that I can no longer understand the DJs. I like some of the songs. But the clue there is in those two little words 'some of'. Time moves on. I may never have been hip, but now I'm even less so. They say that the one constant in life is change. So I take up the challenge of that when it comes to the nature of the Christian faith. And how we communicate it.

Jesus has been adjusting to change ever since Paul took the faith beyond the Jewish world. As soon as those pesky gentiles started getting converted then the language and references had to shift a little. When Paul stood up in Athens he didn't talk about the God of the Old Testament, instead he pointed to their statue of the unknown God, and said those startling words, 'Let me tell you about him.' I don't want to feel threatened by culture shifts, though I may feel increasingly creaky. But I do want to make use of the ever-changing shifts in technology, habits, lifestyles, and worldviews. As much as I can anyway.

Bored and Fed Up

Twenty years ago I was bored, disappointed, confused and fed up. Mostly with myself. Work had not developed as I had hoped, I hadn't become a successful and wealthy author overnight, and no matter how much I bellyached about it, or sent off manuscripts to publishers, I couldn't make it happen. It plunged me into a crisis. And, unafraid of speaking my mind, I complained a lot about church being predictable and boring. I had, to be honest, been bored in services most of my life. Ultimately this crisis set me on a trajectory of doing my level best to make any talks I give more engaging, visual and different. I don't want to give sermons, I want people to experience something. That's my aim anyway. I fall short all the time, of course, but I have a dream. I've come to care about people's experience of church, I fear it still comes across as weird, dull and irrelevant at times. And I'm convinced that Jesus never came across like that. He was earthy, rooted, understandable and entertaining.

Unpredictable

The imaginative and flexible style of Jesus fascinates me. He was never predictable, unlike many of our carefully planned events and services, and I say that as someone who plans these things carefully myself. Life is full of interruptions and complications, I've said that many times, it's a quote from *Love Actually*. Even when Jesus has plans he is willing to go with the interruptions and complications. Like the time he was on his way to heal a dying girl and stopped to name-check a humble stranger in the crowd. To place a hand on the shoulder of this spurned, unloved woman, and look her in the eyes to show her how much she meant to God. It's almost as if he made a ministry out of the interruptions and complications. His travelling was so important to him, often not because of where he was heading, but because of who he met and what happened on the way. So much of his teaching and so many of his conversations were in the context of walking. My journeys are so often about A to B. And while I'm doing them I'm thinking about how soon I can get to C afterwards. And then D beyond that. So I miss the gift of the journey. I allow the pressures and demands to steal the present moment. Not so for Jesus. He knew how to be here and be now. How to make the most of each moment. And when he met folk, whether they were friends, enemies, strangers, or frenemies, he gave them his full attention. They were all that mattered to him at that moment.

Singing

And considering that old nugget about plans and God, do you remember that old joke which goes – how do you make God laugh? Tell him your plans.

Well, there could be some truth in that, especially as life is unpredictable. Parachute into Proverbs chapter 19 v 21 and you'll find we're told that we may make our plans BUT God has the last word. That doesn't mean we shouldn't make plans, dream big dreams, etc. Some of those will work out, some of them won't. It's about flexibility again. We have faith, we have imaginations, we dream, we think, we plan, we're called to people with a vision. And I heard recently that this Proverbs verse can mean – we make our plans AND God has the last word. His plans are ticking over all the time, his purposes continue working their way through and sometimes in spite of our plans. Jesus spoke about doing what he saw his father doing. Or, to draw on a line from the

2018 version of the film *A Star is Born*, God might say to us, 'I'm going to sing my song anyway, all you have to do is trust me and join in.'

Frank Skinner

I used to say that when the children came back from Sunday school, brought in for that last few minutes of church, we could announce 'Here comes the Holy Spirit!' I was being provocative, but deliberately so. Children say the unexpected, inappropriate things. They are curious and questioning and say it like it is. (More on this in a few paragraphs' time.) Recently when my wife was telling our young daughter Lucy about Jesus asking us to forgive our enemies, Lucy said, 'Well that's never gonna happen!' There's a great moment in Frank Skinner's *A Comedian's Prayer Book*, when he suggests that the adults should be the ones leaving the service part way through. Bearing in mind what Jesus says about the kingdom and children, and us sophisticated grown-ups becoming more like them, '...it is the adults who should be led to the door, while the children remain to just believe, on their own terms and through their own sweet filters. Meanwhile mum and dad sit together in the boiled-cabbage backstage of the church, trying to iron the creases out of their faith, to squeeze past the pragmatism, social pressures, and intellectual embarrassment of being a believer in the 21st century.'

Small Boats

I like that. I really do. I mean, I love learning all about the context of the biblical stories and teaching, so I can broaden my understanding. And so develop my appreciation of who

God is and how he cares and communicates. But when the crunch comes to shove, when things fall apart again, and my mental state is untidy and rebellious once more, then I'm just a small boy crying out to God for help and comfort and relief. It's like that old saying about there being no atheists in a small boat on a tornado-tossed ocean. Ultimately I want God to love me and rescue me and help me through each day. That's the heart of it.

Pencil Faith

There's a lovely true story I heard years ago about a young boy in a poor village who couldn't go to school without a pencil. With his rolled-up piece of school paper pressed between his hands he sat by the road and prayed a simple prayer of longing, while he rubbed his hands together. Suddenly the paper felt different, he unrolled it to find a new pencil right there, waiting for him to take to school. Beautiful.

I realise that pencil story might seem a little random, but I love its simplicity. And I'm not saying all prayer is that instant or simple. I just love that story about that boy.

The Mind

I recently stumbled across Paul's famous line about us 'having the mind of Jesus' in 1 Corinthians 2 v 16. My heart sank, because I immediately felt this was beyond my reach. My first thought was about having a nice, clean, tidy mind, and my brain is often like a computer hard drive, full of bad clusters. However, I let this thought rattle around my head for a while, and then something struck me. To find out what the mind of Jesus is about I needed to revisit his life in the gospels, that was surely the best place to see what he was focussed on. And suddenly I began to think differently. It was a bit of a light bulb moment. And so I drew up this list:

Wonder, curiosity, hope, kindness, empathy, courage, ideas, possibilities, compassion, humour, laughter, tears, stories, appreciation, justice, mercy, the present moment, questions…

Not unlike some of the qualities that we find in many children. Not least the ability to ask a million questions. So that set me thinking again – and I realised that Jesus asked a lot of questions, they seemed to be vital to his work…

- Is there no one left to condemn you?
- Why are you crying?
- Who do you say I am?
- Didn't you know I'd be in my father's house?
- Which one was a neighbour?
- Would you give me a drink?
- How many baskets of leftovers?
- My God, my God, why…?
- Why did you doubt me?

Perhaps we should ask more questions and offer less opinions sometimes? Just a thought, says he who is offering a whole book of opinions right here!

Curious

Just to return to children for a moment, and the way Jesus holds them up as a great example of the kingdom. They are curious, questioning, outspoken, random, inquisitive, with no divide between what is considered ordinary and what is supposed to be 'holy'. We pray a night time prayer with our younger daughter, but nine times out of ten it may well be interrupted with a question from her about school, or toys, or clothes or a TV programme. Jesus was a bit like that too. He saw no separation and referenced food, money, work, families, competition and animals in his stories. Anything and everything could be a sign of the kingdom of God in this world. Anything can remind us of the ways and presence of our creator. After all, he is a Creator and he made all the ordinary stuff. Why shouldn't he reference it to help us trust him and get to know him better?

A Moment to Mess About

I have a video recording of our daughter at about seven reading a poem she loved called *I wanna be a bear* by Joshua Seigal. She reads it with great energy and lots of enjoyment. Every so often she coughs and sometimes she has to pause, and her timing isn't always right. Each time she reads the chorus line she reads it louder than the other lines. But at the end she looks at the camera, pulls a big grin and announces her name happily. It's a great video and always brings a smile. She's celebrating a funny poem by reading it to the world with unrestrained gusto.

A while ago a friend sent me a copy of the book *Dangerous Wonder* by Mike Yaconelli. It's an inspiring book about rediscovering our sense of childlike wonder with regards to life, faith, God and the world. And then I watched some of

Ken Robinson's Ted talk *Do Schools Kill Creativity* on YouTube. 'If you're not prepared to be wrong you'll never come up with anything original,' Ken says, 'and by the time we get to be adults we are frightened to be wrong.' Ken describes the way children are not afraid to just have a go. And I know from my own family that little ones all dance, sing, draw, paint, make things up with no fear that it might not be good enough. So I thought I'd shelve my fear for a page or two and have a go at being creative and not fear being wrong, or at least not fear being not so good. Just for the fun of it. Just for a smile. Just to have a go and see what happens. I've written some books that may never sell. A kindle novel about some friends meeting on the day David Bowie died. A film noir adventure based on three money parables of Jesus. A collection of short stories, some just for fun, some with a deeper meaning. A trilogy about an academy for the kids of action heroes. (I actually do know that those three have been read, my older daughter really enjoyed them.) I'm not saying these books are any good, but I enjoyed writing them.

It's about writing just for the fun of it. For the pleasure of telling stories. And in case you want to try something, just over the page you'll find a bunch of blank pages with nothing but borders on them, the rest of it is up to you. Scribble, doodle, write stuff and cross it out again, make it rhyme, make it not rhyme, rant, criticise my poem, add more to my poem, illustrate it. Make a list of possible things you might try one day. Just don't be worried about getting anything right. Not at all. Be wrong. Experiment. No one's watching. Only God and he loves it when we play. So here's a silly poem, a random stream of thoughts which came out like this.

Prophets

I'm not too sure I could be a biblical prophet,
I don't think you can make a good living off it,
And given a plate of locusts I don't think I could scoff it,
Unlike John the Baptist, who seemed to thrive off it,
Who sadly, given a cap could no longer doff it,
'Cause when it came to his head, Herod said 'Off it.'
Scammed by his wife when her daughter danced for profit.
So John shuffled along this mortal coil and promptly fell off
it.
Though his life that day had become a write-off, it
Couldn't destroy the words of this baptising prophet.
So when you next see a locust with honey dripping off it,
Spare a thought for John and every other brave prophet.

Moses

Moses may well have had a stutter
Or perhaps a tendency to mutter
Certainly his heart went aflutter
When a burning bush began to utter
An invitation to go to Calcutta…
Only kidding, it wasn't Calcutta
It was Egypt instead, to see that nutter
Pharaoh who was a complete and utter
Slave driver whose heart was in the gutter
He so burdened the Israelites their legs turned to butter,
So Moses confronted him (no sign of his stutter)
With ten plagues that made him splutter

He eventually gave in and with a growly mutter,
Said 'Let them go! You and your people can cut a
Path to the Red Sea…' but then he changed and did utter
'Get them back! I must have been a nutter
To let them go!' And so he chased them, but er…
He got stuck in the mud and his men began to splutter
As the Red Sea closed over them and their eyelids did flutter.

These poems began life as a list of words that rhyme. Our family compiled it whilst out for a walk one day, we bantered about funny words that rhymed. And later my first attempt at making a poem from some of them went like this:

Tutter, stutter, sputter, shutter, rutter, cutter
At times I feel like a bit of a nutter
When my head and nerves they start to flutter,
When my legs go weak and just turn to butter,
My energy fails and my engines sputter…
And I sometimes find that I'm full of splutter,
When I try to look good and fall in the gutter,
I often think I have wise words, which are so utter-
-ly smart but in truth they're little more than a mutter.

Part 7:

Known and Knowing

Seen

In Genesis 16 Hagar fled into the desert, after she had been used and misused by Abraham and Sarah. She was broken and depressed, and then she met an angel. And in that meeting she discovered something. God saw and knew her. The experience was positive and transformative for her, so much so that she was able to turn around and go home again. Her head held a little higher. And she came back with a name on her lips 'El-roi'. A name she had made up. 'The God who sees me.' And arriving back she freely announced, 'I have seen the One who sees me.' She knew herself to be known and understood, and she is the only person in the Old Testament to give God a name.

When Jesus rescued a Samaritan woman at a well, after she had been dumped by four husbands; when he rescued a woman condemned for her adultery; when he rescued a tax collector stuck up a tree; and when he offered his hand to a fisherman who fell on his face, claiming to be too bad to be a disciple... Jesus saw them all clearly. Knew them for who they were, and in each case he made their lives better. Not worse. When a bunch of excited children came hurtling towards him, feet and hands flying all over the place, he saw them too. Knew their chaotic wonder and exuberance. And he wanted to be close to them. The God who sees us lives on. And he sees and knows and understands each of us today.

Longing

I think that however we put it, whatever phrases we use, we long to be loved and affirmed and accepted. As we are. With or without our tattoos, fashion accessories, hair dye, social media profile, successes, embarrassments or alibis. We just want to know that we are all right and we are known and understood and appreciated and valued. Whatever age, gender, background and personality.

To quote a couple of lines from the song *City of Stars* from the movie *La La Land:* 'Just one thing everybody wants, there in the bars and through the smokescreen of the crowded restaurants... all we're looking for is love from someone else... a voice that says, I'll be here, and you'll be alright.'

No one is immune to the deep longing of our humanity. It affects all we do and are, how we see the world, the future, eternity, each other, ourselves, this moment now. It affects how we treat all these things. What we say and do and believe. It seems to me when I have a sense of my value in God's eyes then I am more at peace and can operate more freely, and be more caring and open. More truly human.

Juggernaut

How can we know this? How do we discover and keep rediscovering this? Not easy or straightforward is it? With all that Jesus faced each day, the pressure, the insults, the demands, the conflict, the decision-making, his calling... it was vital to take time out with his father. In Mark's first action-packed chapter, after a juggernaut of activity, we read that early the next morning Jesus was up and out on his own, refocussing with his father. And when his disciples came hunting for him, with the urgent news that the crowds were back for more, Jesus was unafraid to say 'No' to those demands, and had a plan to move on. I can't help wondering how he felt when, his mind clear, and his soul in harmony with his father, he heard those hurried pounding steps of the friends who had come to find him, just when he'd found space and peace to re-centre himself on God, the demands crashed in again. Just when he'd been able to grab some time with his father, his brothers and sisters were invading his space once more.

R&R

In John chapter 13 v 3 we uncover something deeply significant.

Jesus wasn't insecure.

John assures us that Jesus knew where he'd come from, where he was going, and who he was in this world. That's how he could cope with all he was carrying and encountering. *Jesus knew that the Father had given him authority over everything and that he had come from God and would return to God.* So John writes in verse 13. Jesus was never needing to prove himself, or assert his authority, or demand his own way. He never needed to do anything for show or to prove himself. Or big himself up. He knew his place in God. And he kept renewing that vision each morning out in quiet wilderness, free places. Vital time out. Nourishing R&R.

Feet on the Ground

So when Jesus washed his disciples' feet it wasn't about him. Not at all. Though it could have been.

'Right you lot, listen up, can you all see what I'm doing here? Well move then Matthew so you can get a proper view. Now, I've got a bowl full of water, can anyone guess what an extraordinary thing I'm about to do? No Thomas I'm not about to throw it over Judas. Pay attention will you. Well, move closer if you need to. Now look at what I'm doing. Look! See? See Peter's feet, see these appalling examples of walking gear? I'm gonna wash 'em. Yes, I am! Ohhhhh… yes I am!!! Extraordinary isn't it? Humble, aren't I? I mean look at 'em, look at what they're covered in, look at what he's stepped in, have you seen how bad they are underneath? And what they smell like? Plus I don't think he's cut his nails since the Romans invaded. Or seen a chiropodist. Appalling, aren't they? And yet… and yet Andrew, me, yes little old me, I'm going to kneel down and do the job of the lowest slave. Oh yes, I am. Aren't you impressed? Matthew, eyes on me please. No fidgeting or looking at your iScroll, okay? No James, you can't have a loo break. This is too important now. I want everybody to take note, and John, write this one down for your new book. And I want it in bold and underlined. Okay?'

Nope.

He was nothing like that. And as I mentioned before, John recorded why, and to paraphrase it in my words, he said this:

'Jesus knew who he was, he knew he could do anything, and had all the power in the world. He knew his father had given him everything, and he was clearsighted about where he had come from and where he was going. So, he was able to take a towel and a bowl and kneel and wash his disciples' feet…'

You could say he'd been washing feet all his life really, serving the world. With nothing to prove. Firmly rooted in his father, and only concerned to draw us closer to the one who made us and has all the compassion in the universe for us. So that we might glimpse who we are, where we've come from, and where we are going.

Chariots

I guess it works differently for each of us. I'm not an orderly person, I struggle to have an established quiet time each day. But I have discovered a way of re-centring on God with a few seconds silence at random points throughout the day, just stopping wherever I am, quieting my spirit and simply taking a moment to appreciate God with me in that moment. Slowing myself down to appreciate God with me in the now. A friend of mine says that God is always present, the problem is, I am not. Our heads get crammed with to-do lists, or whether we got things right in the past, or our fears for the future. Of course they do, it's the human way. To quote a line from the film *Chariots of Fire* – 'Your head's so full of running there's no room for standing still.' So we need help to stop and calm ourselves, to reconnect.

Crowded

I'm aware that this may not be easy for us. Our minds can crowd with destructive or unhelpful thoughts when we try and clear them for a moment. So maybe a line from a psalm could help, just holding onto something like that?

There are so many verses in the Bible about calming ourselves, the most famous is in Psalm 46 and verse 10:
'Be still and know that I am God.'
But these verses are spattered all over the Psalms.

Psalm 37 v 7: Be still before the LORD and wait patiently for him…

Psalm 62 v 5: Find rest, O my soul, in God alone; my hope comes from him.

Psalm 131 v 2: I have stilled and quieted my soul; like a small child with its mother…

Something Small

It's possible that moments of stillness like this affect our saying and doing for the rest of the day. The quiet we invest in, a few seconds at time, affects the hours of living that follow it. God is on our side, but so many influences and news stories and opinions can be like the white noise of radio interference, getting in the way of us receiving the good news of God with us. The good news that we are thoroughly known by him. Try just stopping now. Taking a pause. Look out the window, notice something small that is good. Just for five seconds. And remind yourself of the presence of God with you. It's not about needing to say anything, to ask for anything, or promise anything. It's just stopping and honouring him with nothing but five seconds of your time. Five seconds of your uncluttered presence blended with God's presence. A reminder in the silence that he's on your side. He cares about you and for you. He understands your fears and foibles and failings, your hope and dreams and desires. Here's a gap so you can do that. Right now. Doesn't have to be for long, set the bar low so you can reach it. Aim at this in such a way that you cannot fail. Try it for a few seconds now. Here's a gap in time offered for you to do it now…

A Gap For Being Still For a Few Seconds

This One

You may or may not sense something. You may well find your head immediately fills up with things you need to do. Good ideas. Bright ideas. Things you've forgotten. Coffee you can drink. Snacks you can eat. An app you can look at on your phone. I get that all the time. The moment I stop I think of so many reasons to start again. But it's only for a few seconds. And it's something you can do anywhere. Walking, working, shopping, standing, sitting, lying down. In the rain and the sun and the snow. Outside and in. Obviously best not to try it in the middle of a conversation. The other person may start to worry about you. But there are plenty of other opportunities and the beauty of it is, you don't need anything to make it happen. It's free and requires no equipment. You see, to press home the point for a moment...

God is with you in this moment now.

Right here. Right now. As you hold this book.

And he's with you in this moment...

And in this moment...

And in this one...

And in this one...

And this one...

And this one...

And this one...

And this one...

And this one...

And this one...

And this one...

And this one...

And this one...

And this one...

And this one...

And this one...

And this one...

And this one...

And this one...

And this one...

And this one...

And this one...

And this one...

I think I've made my point.

Looking

When Jesus tried to encourage his disciples not to worry, he told them, in Matthew 6 v 25–34, to take a look at the flowers and the birds, bits of creation if you like. And it seemed to me he was telling them to take a moment to refocus on a snapshot, a meme, of God and his creativity with us. So I wrote this piece as a kind of reminder about that:

The Penguin

'Don't worry…' we are told.

If only.

But Jesus tells us more, offers us something else.

Go and find something green, he suggests.

Something that flies, or sings, or blossoms.

Something that drifts in the breeze.

Something that moves a little slowly.

Consider the robins, the skies, the worms, the daisies.

Birds do of course come a cropper,

And fall from the skies (Jesus tells us this),

And the grass withers and flowers fade…

But in going outside, or looking through glass,

To these things of creation,

To things, bigger, smaller, brighter, quirkier…

We lift our minds for a time,

Take them from our worries,

From the mess and chaos and uncertainty,

And offer them to our creator.

Jesus isn't just saying,

'Don't think of the elephant in the room,'
But rather… 'Ooh look! There's a penguin!'
Offering us something else to fill our thoughts,
Something to help us focus our minds again on him.

Talking

A while ago someone told me about the saying that 'silence is the first language of God', so that set me thinking too. Are we so used to people talking at us that we expect God to communicate with lots of talk as well? And so with that in mind I came up with these few lines:

Language

The first language of God is silence.
Not success,
Or victory,
Or popularity,
Or power.

The first language of God is silence.
Not a clamouring,
Or a shouting,
A vying for attention,
Or a desperate plea to be picked.

The first language of God is silence.
Though we may wish otherwise,
Long for a dramatic monologue,
Or a tender whisper.

Instead…

The silence of a corpse on a cross,

And a pre-resurrection tomb.

The silence of a lone figure in the wilderness,

A rabbi praying in the early morning,

And a creation waiting for that first stirring word.

In the quiet of every moment when

You and I think that nothing is going on…

The first language of God is silence.

Dialects

'God made their hearts, so he understands everything they do.'

The verse above is tucked neatly into Psalm 133 v 15. And it made me think about the different ways God speaks to different people. I like the way it suggests that God knows what best connects with each of us and is able to use all kinds of ordinary things to connect with us, to reassure us, to challenge and inspire us. So I wrote this reading about the way God speaks in many ways, depending on what works for each of us:

God Speaks a Billion Dialects

I am struck today by this contrary gospel

that is both tender and dangerous,

intimate and shocking, edgy and ordinary.

It must be both, for life is both,

and people are both.

And the gospel is as real and relevant and present
for the trowel-wielding, cement-spattered builder,
up their ladder with their industrial strength tea;
as it is real and relevant and present
for the waif-like ballet dancer,
on tiptoes, in their pristine costume,
concerned about keeping their figure just the right size.
The good news must be
real and relevant and present to us all,
for God speaks a million languages
and a billion dialects and it is just plain daft
to suppose he does not.
And if the grace we so desperately need is to be
seared into our being, etched into our minds,
and tattooed onto our hearts,
then God surely understands each one of us,
and knows very well the language we speak.

Reminders

When our older daughter first went off to university I didn't empty the bin in her room for weeks. It probably sounds daft but it reminded me of her presence with us. It made me think she was still somehow in the room. Of course I did empty it eventually. And she came back and filled it again. I also remember my dad keeping my mum's handbag in place beside her chair long after she had died. I think many people do this kind of thing. Physical reminders of the person they love.

Aroma

Some friends told me recently about their visit to London during the time of mourning for Queen Elizabeth's death. They mentioned something that you couldn't pick up from the TV coverage – the scent of the flowers. Many people had placed flowers around the trees, and they were filling the air with a magnificent fragrance. And that reminded me of the time Jesus was anointed in Bethany, by his friend Mary, and the way that aroma must have filled the house for days afterwards. The scent of God permeating the atmosphere. Most likely continuing on into the events that followed. Throughout the time of the last supper, the arrest and anguish in Gethsemane, then the fake trial and the callous condemnation and crucifixion. Throughout all of that the home in Bethany of Mary, Martha and Lazarus would have been filled with the aroma of hope. A reminder of the presence and friendship of Jesus. And it was still present no doubt on that Sunday morning when the ground trembled and sighed a little, when angels got busy and lulled grave guards to sleep. When the unexpected scrape of a rolling stone gave way to the yawn of an open tomb. Which in turn gave way to the yawning figure of a resurrected carpenter. Stretching and smiling as he walked free of death, with the keys of life in his fist.

Jigsaw Bits

We need reminders of God with us. I carry a tiny wooden cross in my pocket and sometimes when I'm taking a few seconds stillness I take a hold of it. It is full of names of those I pray for, printed in a tiny font and stuck on. (God has very good eyesight.) It reminds me of God with me and it's a way of offering all those people to him. I sometimes give out jigsaw pieces when I speak at events, reminders that we are part of the picture God is putting together in the world. Vital jigsaw lives, all different, all unique, all chosen. Not because we are brilliant, but because he is good. We can't control the big picture, but we can play our part. Sometimes in surprising ways.

There is a moment in Galatians chapter 1 v 18 when Paul reveals something interesting. The first time he went to Jerusalem, three whole years after his conversion, he stayed for a fortnight with Peter. At this stage Paul has been a Christian for three years, studying what we now call the Old Testament, finding Jesus in all those Hebrew writings. But he's not yet read any of the gospel stories (he can't, they haven't been written). And then he goes to Jerusalem. And stays with Peter and his wife. And effectively he encounters and absorbs what would become Mark's gospel.

Peter tells him all about Jesus – his miracles, his encounters, his relationships, his sayings, his conversations, his stories, his lifestyle. Suddenly Paul has access to Jesus via someone who lived beside him for three years. And the rough and ready, gritty, impetuous fisherman becomes a vital mentor to the refined, privileged and educated scholar. Peter disciples Paul! Who knew? Extraordinary. Two very different pieces of God's big jigsaw placed side by side for 15 days. And presumably neither were ever the same again.

And they did have one thing common. The kind of thing we all have in common. Messing up. Falling short. Missing the target. Failure. Mistakes. Peter had abandoned Jesus on that terrible Gethsemane night. Paul had set his heart on destroying people like Peter. Both experienced that fresh-start forgiveness that Jesus carries in his scarred hands.

Part 8:

The Longest Pause in History

400 years. Waiting, wondering, a gap in history, Malachi and his visionary promises now just a dot on the skyline in the rear-view mirror. 400 years. Generations rising and falling. Babies born, weaned, schooled, trained, married, reproducing, growing old, wearing out and dying. Over and over. A tumbling of the years. And meanwhile a young indomitable Greek comes along, ambition in his clenched fists, and a common language takes hold. 400 years. And another empire stretches and rises and takes the land. And the Caesars hail themselves gods, king of kings, lord of lords and princes of peace. Worthy of the people's honour and praise. Or so they claim. A peace forged with spears and swords and crosses. 400 years. More births and burials. A catalogue of questions and barely holding on. When? When? When? And meanwhile the Caesars get their men building roads, and travel takes off. A flurry of movement and migration across the empire. And in a small Bethlehem backwater, on a silent night, a first-time mother cries and gasps and clutches at her husband. And in a field nearby peace on earth is announced. And shepherds run, and wise men saddle up, and an old couple in the temple catch their breath, believing that the king will come. 400 years. And the world shifts. And an exhausted young woman cradles her baby in the night, and alongside the wonder and relief and heart-bursting joy, she feels the first fierce nip of a sword piercing her heart.

Luke 2 & the blank page between the two testaments

Part 9:
Scenes from a Galilean Revolution

How the Revolution Began

A young woman, mid-teens, carries water from the well. The usual job, sweat runs down from her neck to the small of her back. Her stomach flutters a little, as if invaded by butterflies. Or something else. There is no ultrasound, no clinic where she might discover the truth of the life she carries, but soon she will know. A wingless, halo-free angel will knock on her door, tower above her, smile and tell her not to worry. Not to be afraid. She's a woman of the impossible, a woman to shake the world, a woman carrying a creator in her flesh. A baby. Tiny as yet, but forming, growing, kicking as the months pass. She may be a second-class citizen in her world, but she will be a first-class mother. And every citizen, whatever class, will have their world remade because she was willing to say a dry-throated, stomach fluttering yes. And soon she must face the ire of the village and the shame of her family. None of them able to imagine that their God could be big enough to do things his own way. To step aside from the safe lines of life, in order to choose a young woman, and her aging cousin, to birth a double-act that will challenge every rule in the book, every notion of #this-is-how-we've-always-done-it. A new thing. A better way. A road not travelled. Till now.

Luke 1 vv 26–38

Clean

A man scoops water from a huge jar. He pours it into a cup and tastes it. Frowns. Something is wrong. He scoops some more and tastes that. This is strange. He takes the cup to another man, hands it to him. The other man looks terrified but as soon as he drinks from the cup his face relaxes. He laughs, has to take another sip, then a large gulp. He laughs again, his eyes wide with wonder. He urges the first man to fetch more cups of water and start passing them out. Before long the place is buzzing. The party had come to an uncertain standstill but now everything has changed. There is laughter, dancing, celebration once more. A surge of warmth and wonder. A burst of life as if a river of living water has resurrected a few things. But the first man, his job done, returns to the huge jar. If this water has changed, if as it seems it's become vintage wine, what will they use for purification now? This water was supposed to be there for cleansing. How will they get clean now? How will they get renewed, become acceptable to God now? And behind him, not too far away, a carpenter notices his concern and smiles.

John 2 vv 1–12

The Man on the Floor

A man leans over another man, they are in a cramped environment. Bodies everywhere. The place smells of sweat and fistfuls of snack food, dates and fish wrapped in flatbread. Dust trickles down from a gap in the roof, four faces bash against each other, each trying to get a better look down inside. The man who leans over says something about forgiveness and the cramped room is full of gasps, so much so that the place feels twice as cramped. The other man, lying twisted on the floor starts to cry. He didn't expect forgiveness. His mind is blown, and he feels a burden lift from his past. The man leaning over him says something else and offers a hand. The man on the floor doesn't need a second offer, he takes the hand, grips it so tightly all the knuckles turn white. His own and the man offering his hand. There is a grunt and groan and the scrabbling of feet and the man on the floor is now a man upright and jumping and twisting a kind of salvation groove, a dance of unexpected freedom. The room is filled with so many gasps now it feels as if the walls might burst. The man pushes his way through the crowd and nose-dives out of the door. He goes gyrating and laughing and crying down the street. And a houseful of people follow him, not just one man receives his legs back, but everyone has a chance to, and a reason, to dance again.

Mark 2 vv 17–26

An Offered Hand

A woman falls heavily, awkwardly in the dirt, twisting her ankle as she sprawls, bits of grit biting into her hands and knees, scraping the skin away, embedding themselves and drawing blood. A group of men surround her, sneering, baying for gore, wallowing in their snide remarks and lewd accusations. There are trails of spit in her hair, not from a lover's kiss, but from the snarls of haters. Yet there's another man in the circle, near her, on her side, sitting there, waiting, watching, calmly patient for the moment when he will interject and offer the thugs a rock-dropping reply. The kind of reply that will lift the woman's head and restore a glimmer of hope in her heart. The kind of reply that will mean the murderous gang will dissipate back into their sterile lives of blame. The kind of reply that will come with an offered hand and a warm, forgiving smile. And while he waits he writes in the dust, the names of those accusing her, the names of those who have themselves strayed in many ways at many times. And when the thudding from the discarded rocks has fallen silent, and when the sound of their receding footsteps is no more, he will ask her his own question, one that offers a brighter future. And when the woman stands, the grit will fall from her wounds, and her ankle will be twisted no more. She will walk away into a new kind of life. This is the nature of it. Another untidy encounter. Another life dismantled and reconstructed.

John 8 vv 1–11

The Casket

A mother who is no longer a mother, a wife no longer a wife, walks beside a casket, mourners wail and weep but perhaps she is so empty she doesn't even have tears inside her now. She's in some ways dead too, inside. Her husband has gone and now here she is saying goodbye to her son. A man watches and instead of keeping a safe distance he decides to invade her space, steps suddenly towards the casket, a gentle lunge, a hand stretched as if waking a sleeping child, only the child is a man and he's not sleeping. In spite of this he stirs, blinks, splutters, groans, yawns, coughs, stretches, scratches, sniffs and sits up. The woman gasps, a mother again, and the tears now do manage to flow, happiness has brought her back from the dead. Just as her son now flexes and clambers, and then falls from the coffin. Nothing dignified about it, clumsy, awkward, inappropriate for a funeral, the corpse splayed on the ground for a moment before he leaps up and hugs his mother. And the onlookers aren't sure what just happened. But the man, the other man, the space invader, he nods at the mother, smiles at the son.

And though the world had seemed to stop for a while, somehow, miraculously, it is turning again.

Luke 7 vv 11–15

Small

A woman loiters at the back of a crowd. She is small, insignificant. She doesn't smell good. She is frightened of crowds, because they are frightened of her. She moves to push through, then pulls back again. She thinks. Bites her chapped lip. She moves again, spots a gap and slips inside, like a snake slithering between two rocks. She does everything possible to avoid alerting others to her presence, but still they glance sideways. Her rag clothes brush against robes and dresses. Her bloodied feet carrying her hunched and decaying form through the bustling waves of bodies. It feels odd to be amongst so much life after so much death. Two opposites will soon collide, but the collision will be soft, warm, uplifting. The man in the crowd, the man who is the cause of the crowd, will reach down, lift her up, cradle her mottled face in his hand, look her in the eyes and call her by name. Address her as a precious daughter of God. Things no one has done in 12 years. She will never be the same. And we may not be too. One woman has been pulled from the jaws of death, and the rest of us are offered a new chance of living.

Mark 5 vv 21–34

Begging

A man begs by a gate, another man passes by. The sun rises and falls, the image on fast play. He begs by the gate again. The other man passes by. The sun rises and falls, rises and falls, a never-ending cycle of cold and heat, dark and light, shivering and sweat. Then the never-ending stops. The man begging is just a bag of bones. His skin rots and his meagre muscles wither away. The man passing by abruptly clutches at his own chest, staggers, lunges for the gatepost where the beggar's clothes lie tattered and empty now. A few bones protruding from the meagre pile. The other man falls, his face contorted, and drops on top of the beggar's bones. He melts into the floor, and keeps on falling, down and down to the bottom of the world, and lower, beyond the bottom of the world. The light fades, the atmosphere becomes thick with darkness. Now he's in a cavern, looking upwards towards another kind of light. There he sees the beggar, no beggar now though. He has more than enough. He's feasting and no longer alone. The other man still clutches at his chest and calls out, something about needing help. His world, once bright and full of life, now merely gloomy, cobwebbed and decaying. He calls out again and a conversation ensues. He wants the beggar to bring him sustenance. But there's a gap, a ravine, blocking the way. Crossing is out of the question. The beggar is now a king, a celebrity, lifted up from the dust and restored to life. The last has become first, the least the greatest, the dirtiest the cleanest, the rejected welcome, the side-lined centre stage. Blessed are the poor in spirit, those who struggle, those who are full of worries and questions, those who are not the brightest and best, those who know they need God, for theirs is the kingdom of heaven. And the teller of this tale smiles as he finishes, knowing that one day he will give every ounce of his being, sinking shipwrecked into the foulest, darkest sea, for the troubled and the misfits and the square-peg-round-hole people.

Luke 16 vv 19–31

The Curtain

Three men stare at three other men. The scene is almost blinding, the light is dazzling. The three men watching have their mouths wide open. The three others are talking. Not long ago one of the men watching had declared that they were spending time with the son of God. Now here he is, on this mountain, so bright that the world can barely cope. The other two dazzling men shouldn't be here. It's impossible. They are long gone, two prophets from an ancient past. And yet here they are, in animated conversation, three shining heroes, discussing something from the past, or maybe something about the future. One of the men watching figures this is the way it's all going to end now, up here, with a glimpse of heaven. So let's build a home and stay here forever. No need to venture back down towards the mess and conflict and gloom of life on earth. Yet even as he suggests this a cloud appears from nowhere, a curtain dropping as if to end the scene. And there's a voice in the sky, a bit like thunder, 'This is my son, my great son. I love him completely, and I'm proud of him. Listen to what he tells you.' And when the curtain rises once more for the second act two of the shining figures have disappeared and there's only the one man left, and he looks normal again. No spotlight glare or stadium beams shining on him now. No inner glow. Just the son of God with skin on, and he's starting to walk back down hill, back to reality. Back to the mess and the conflict and the gloom. Surely not. Not when he could swap all that for the wonder and the glory up here. Not when he could stay up here and avoid all the pressure and stress and conflict. But no. He's on his way back to earth. The three men watching had fallen on their faces when the voice boomed from the sky. But now he's urging them to stand up again and follow him, telling them not to be afraid. And they trudge back down the mountain to the urgent call and the chaotic ways of reality.

Matthew 17

The Missed Commandment

A teacher watches another man fade into the distance. That second man comes to a crossroads, stands for a moment deciding which way to choose. This has been a key day for him, a day he will think about every morning when he wakes. He has a big house, servants, his life drips with opulence. He has everything he wants. And yet nothing he needs. The mountain of everything he has is big enough to blot out the questions about what he needs, but every so often those questions rise again. And every so often he remembers that man, and that day, and that conversation. That day he listened to the commandments from the teacher with the insightful gaze. The one who seemed to look into him the way no one else ever had. Those commandments which made life work. So wise. So practical. He knew them so well.

And yet there was an omission. The teacher had missed one, the one about coveting. About wanting more things. About craving, building an empire of stuff. And he knew now, the teacher had hoped he might spot the one not mentioned. Point it out. But he didn't. He couldn't. Might open up a difficult conversation, turn the spotlight on the nature of his heart and mind. And so he wakes each morning and remembers, and in remembering he sees the teacher's face once more. That insightful gaze, no condemnation in it, just invitation. And an open smile. And he senses the offer

116

still stands, and that even today he could return to that crossroads and take another way.

Mark 10 vv 17–22

Dry Hearts

A man looks out over a huge crowd. So many bodies, so many faces, so much alike. And yet he sees more. He sees hopes and dreams and illness and longing. He sees regret and sorrow, loss and tragedy. And he sees desires and visions and hidden strength. So many faces, so many people. To anyone else this would be just another crowd, to him it's a home for another kingdom; a thousand dry hearts, thirsty for some living water. He sees another world here, another realm, a life less ordinary, tailormade for those who know they need more, those who society has pushed aside, those who slip between the cracks, those who turn no heads when they walk in the room. Those who have lost homes, income, family, land, work, direction, hope, friends, health, purpose. These are his people. Humble, wandering, hungry, oppressed, grieving. And the kingdom is among them.

Matthew 5 vv 3–10, Luke 17 vv 21–22

Unholy

A group of men who think they know everything stare at a man who clearly doesn't. Their faces are grim masks. Occasionally one or two look as if they are raising an astonished eyebrow, or cracking a gentle smile, but no. They are here to be unimpressed. If this uneducated upstart keeps on this road much longer it will end up being a short one. And there'll be no coming back from it. He dares to challenge them, to insult them, calling them filthy drinking cups rinsed on the outside, but never properly cleansed. As if! They know all about cleansing, thanks very much, they spend their life staying away from anything that might contaminate. He also dares to accuse them of being… mutter it in horrified disbelief… whitewashed tombs! Pristine and ordered on the outside, dead on the inside. Referencing Ezekiel no doubt and the flimsy walls with no strength, made to look strong with a few dabs of paint. How dare he? Charlatan! What does he know anyway? They are the experts round here and yet he's daring to tell them to turn around, to think again, to choose another way. These men have devoted their lives to God and his laws. How can he expect to have any integrity with the way he talks and acts? Look at him. Right now. Making excessive contact with people who are plainly criminals and do-badders. Eating their food, laughing at their jokes, listening to their stories, drinking their wine. How can he ever expect to be taken seriously as a holy man when so much of his life is spent with the unholy. They say he can touch what is unacceptable and make it new, take what is broken and make it whole. But that's not good enough. They need him to acknowledge them, to show a little humility, and bow before their authority. They need him to look to them, to recognise their pride is far more precious than his crowd-pleasing compassion. He needs to clean up his act and start again. Forget his aspirations about being a man of the people, for the people. He needs to step away from them and clean up his act. Otherwise that short road ahead will lead to a dead end.

Ezekiel 13 vv 10–15, Matthew 23 vv 25–28

Wrestling

There's a woman wrestling with a jar of water at a well. She sweats and she doesn't smell too good. It's not her fault, this is the hottest time of the day. She's totally focussed on the water jar, partly because it is heavy, and partly to avoid the eyes of the man sitting nearby. She's had enough scandal in her life, doesn't need more gossip about consorting with a Jew out here on her own. She wouldn't be on her own, sweating out here if it weren't for the other gossip, and the women who spread it. But there you go. There isn't usually anyone else here around now, so this is not what should be happening, not the plan at all. She can hear footsteps, the stranger's approaching her. She tenses up. Hurries to finish. He's speaking, asking her for something. That can't be right. He's supposed to keep his distance. He's still talking, she steels herself, puts on a wry smile and looks at him. Her face is softer, even when the smiling is wry.

'You want a drink?' she says, 'from me? Really? I mean – Really!? From me?'

He nods and says please.

She looks astonished. Jews don't come anywhere near Samaritans like her. How can he have a drink from her if he won't touch the jar? Does he expect her to pour it into his mouth somehow?

'Where's your bucket,' she snaps, 'surely you travel with one?'

He nods, yes. But his friends have gone into the nearby town and taken it with them. So he's in trouble in this heat, vulnerable. Needs her help. Says please again.

She sighs. Men. She's had a bellyful of them. Never to be trusted. Divorced too many times, dumped by too many of them. So many cracks in her heart you can see daylight through it.

She takes her cup and pours him some water. Now he's smiling, and there's a light in his eyes. What's that about? Better keep her distance, and he'd better only be looking for water from her. He cradles his hand around the cup as if it's the best drink he's ever had. Says thank you to her. But then he starts talking about something else. A gift from God, on offer for her.

Her smile broadens. She's known too many men who told her they were God's gift. But hold on, he's not finished.

'If you ask me I can give you living water.'

What's that mean? Living water? He's saying something more. Apparently it never runs dry.

'I'll take some of that then,' she quips, 'wouldn't have to keep coming here in this heat.'

She throws in a few comments about Samaritans versus Jews. Broad hints about how she's right and therefore he's no doubt wrong. But he won't take the bait. In fact, oh great, he's started in on her again. Asking personal questions.

'Why don't you bring your husband and I'll tell you both about the living water?'

She freezes and her world shifts a little. The ground feels unsafe. Keep your mouth shut girl, no need to be honest with this foreign stranger.

'I don't have a husband,' she says, immediately letting loose too much.

And then he does something extraordinary, tells her what he could never have known. Five husbands. Those five ogres who made her feel small and worthless. Yes, he's right. She has had five husbands. And the wounds are still bloody and

120

raw. Five selfish men who just want their women for sex, babies and water. She was always too opinionated for them, thought too deeply, spoke too much. Divorce, divorce, divorce, divorce, divorce. Time after time. Like a hail of cruel stones bruising and cutting deeply. There are some mornings she can barely get out of bed.

She tries to distract him again, pull him away from all this painful stuff. Talks about the well and Jacob and how she is right and he is misguided. But he's not misguided. He knows the man she lives with is not her husband. How? How can he know that? And something begins to stir. Something she knows well. Something she dare not even believe.

'When the Messiah comes,' she says quietly, almost to herself, 'he will tell us everything.'

She knows that because of Moses and his writings in Deuteronomy – 'A prophet will rise up and tell you everything you need to know. I the Lord will tell him what to say. Listen to him!'

Closer. He's coming closer, she freezes, part of her wants to run, another part dare not miss this moment.

'You see who you're talking to?' he says gently, and she risks a glance at his face, 'you know who is speaking to you now? I'm the one you're waiting for; can you see that?'

She can, and her eyes burst wide now. She laughs and then clamps a hand to her mouth, but then she laughs again. Louder, and there are tears on her face too. Laughing and crying all at the same time. Something's happening inside her, some poison draining away. As if she is being washed clean, as if the rejection and the belittling are finding a kind of balm. She begins to back away, spilling water from her jar as she goes. He nods and she laughs again, leaves the jar, and turns to run back to her village. And when she gets there it'll be living water she spills, and the people will come streaming back. Amazed that she is suddenly talking about her past, about everything that's happened to her. All those things she was embarrassed about. She's different and they want to know why. So they follow her, chattering questions and theories as they come. And maybe in that jostling crowd there are even one or two of those men who hurt her. Certainly all the gossiping women are there. But new life is in the air, and she wants them to get a breath of it.

Deuteronomy 18 v 15, John 4 vv 1–30

Rumours

Interesting rumours are floating around. There's a kind of anticipation in the air. One might almost dare to call it hope. People are starting to notice something about this man, there are times when he's looking a bit like some of those old prophets. As if he's doing impressions or something. Just like Elijah and Elisha he's raising dead people. Like Moses he's on the side of a mountain with instructions for a different way of life. And like Moses again he's feeding people with miracle bread and then taking command of the sea. And then there are his visions of the future and his random references to the mysterious son of man, harking back to Daniel. An eternal, global king. He recites the psalms as he juggles a couple pebbles and conjures an image of a stone that was thought worthless, turning out to be the most vital of all. The foundation for everything. And what was it Isaiah said about a future prince of peace with a government resting on his shoulders? Thankfully though he's not been wounded, not been whipped and beaten and led away to die, like a lamb to the slaughter. Nor buried like a criminal in a rich man's grave. No one wants that, that wouldn't be good news. That isn't what anybody needs. That would be nothing but failure.

For now he's certainly reminding them of the old heroes, which makes him look like a new hero. A different leader. And now here he is, riding into town on that donkey... righteous and victorious, just like Zechariah said. That's what they want, signs of the old days of strength and independence, maybe the tide is going to turn. A new king David in town. Perhaps they should sharpen their knives and flex their fists and wait for his call to join the revolution.

Daniel 7 vv 13–14, Psalm 118 v 22, Isaiah 8 v 6, Isaiah 53

Lonely

He often feels lonely, isolated and misunderstood. Sometimes the burden of the world weighs so heavy, feels so bleak, so tortuous, it's as if his soul is dipped in acid and stretched to breaking point. There's so much he is bringing to the world, so much held within his being, how can anyone else ever perceive what he is carrying. And the conflict... oh the conflict... every day more conflict. Stress upon stress upon stress. The misunderstanding of friends, the insults of enemies, the challenges from strangers and the criticism from hardened hearts.

And so he slips away. To this desert place. Alone. While the sun still sleeps and the dawn is yet to break. To tune in once more, to hear again the tender voice of his father. To know himself and his mission once more. To gain a whole other perspective. To be refuelled, recharged for another day of serving and washing feet. Walking the path of obedience. And it's worth it. Every time he sees someone come alive, every time he watches someone recover from years of hurt and loss, every time he sees fresh light dawning, and the flame of hope rekindled. A life rebooted, a spirit revived, a body regenerated. That's what he's here for, that's what he's all about. Those tell-tale signs of rebirth in the smiles and grateful nods, as he joins in with the song his father is always singing. That resurrection song.

Isaiah 53 v 3, Luke 5 v 16, John 5 v 19

Sorrow

He is heartbroken. His cousin. Gone. The one who appointed him. The one who first saw him for who he was, unafraid to announce it to the crowds. Steel in his eyes and fire in his cheeks. The one who affirmed him with a baptism and a word of encouragement. Gone. A foreshadowing perhaps of things to come. He misses his step for a moment. Stops to steady himself. He can't help thinking about the powers that be, those who, twisted in their own thinking, wield their obscene power. Despair comes at him washing over like a sudden Galilean sea-storm. He needs to be alone, needs to let his grief settle, needs to pour out his pain to his father.

And yet, even as his steps slow to a trudge, he starts to hear the cries, the banter and the pounding feet. The people are coming once more, desperate for a way out, calling for him. Anxious for his time and energy. He feels his body slump a little. Can he cope? Can he do this? And as he stands there and sees the craving scrawled large on the faces, he senses his spirit quicken. His father is at work here, and the life begins to wash through him once more. There is still the music of grief playing in the background of his mind, but another song calls him on. These people need feeding, and he won't let them go hungry.   *Matthew 14 v 1-14*

The Precious Girl

A little girl loiters on the edge of the crowd, she is fascinated by this man telling stories. There is a light in his eyes, and he smiles a lot as he walks about, acting out what he is saying. She's never quite seen anyone like him before. She'd love to get closer, but she is shy. Plus she's supposed to keep out of the way. No one attaches any importance to little girls round here. She turns to walk away when a movement catches her eye, the man is waving to her, smiling at her, and beckoning her over. Will she go? Dare she go? In front of this crowd? She takes a little step, notices how scuffed and dusty her old sandals are, she feels suddenly scruffy. But he beckons to her again, so she takes another step. And another. And another. Now he can reach her and has taken her by the hand. He turns her to look at everyone. Some of the people seem confused, some look happy, some look annoyed. What has she done? What did she get wrong? Now he's telling them about her, about how important she is, how precious and special, and about how they should learn from her if they want to know about his new kingdom. And if they want to discover more of God. No one's ever said that before and she's not quite sure she understands it, but as she starts to slip away she feels like a star. Just as she goes she hears her name and turns to see the man nodding to her, thanking her. Wow! she thinks, he knows my name!

Matthew 18 vv 1–6

Precious Women

A group of women count money. Women from quite different backgrounds, and yet here they are, brought together, trusting each other. Some of them count carefully for cash is a scarce commodity. One of them though is very wealthy indeed. They have pooled their resources and now they will play their vital part in the kingdom of God. They pass the funds to the man with the purse. In the background another man notices, nods and gives them the broadest of smiles. They have made his day. They are going down in history. It is because of them that this smiling man can roam freely, bringing good news to the downtrodden, lifting up the broken. Sharing his life, without the need to keep running back to his carpentry shop. And not just him but the man carrying the purse too. And the other men here. The women look at their weathered faces and have to pinch themselves. They never imagined this would happen. Not one of them dreamt of being a disciple as a little girl. How could they? It was beyond imagining. But here they all are. Followers on the Messiah's Road, stepping into the tracks of this man from Nazareth, their sandals spattered with the dust of this rabbi. Learning, growing, experiencing things that usually only men get to experience. But not with this teacher. Here they are welcome, and here they are vital. Mary, Salome, Martha, Susanna, Joanna. And so many others.

Luke 8 vv 1–3

Charred

Restless streets, market traders and vendors jostle for attention. Glistening, frowning figures weave their way between one another in a desperate hurry to live, to survive, to get by, to make it through another day. A people hurting and insecure, quick to judge and in a hurry to prove themselves right. The sound of endurance rises like an out of practice orchestra tuning up. And not merely from this people in this moment now, but down the ages and across the nations.

In a yard nearby a charred mother hen is collapsed in a blackened heap while the owner peels back the layers of its wings to free the chicks hiding for cover underneath. Saved from the fire, alive and breathing and bewildered, and wondering what happened.

And the wisest man who ever lived stands in the midst of all this, watching, absorbing, feeling the pain, sensing the longings. His eyes as clear as day, his heart shot through with compassion. To him this is no faceless, seething mass, but every footstep, every heartbeat is known and noted. If only these precious people knew what made for peace. If only they could see who is standing among them, with them, on their side. If only they would pause long enough for him to gather them under his wings. Before long there will be a fire, and he will stand and take it, his surrendered arms outstretched between the people and the fallout from their rebellion. And on that day, in those dark hours, he will offer room to shelter, room to be saved, space and opportunity to start living again. He wipes his eyes.

Matthew 23 v 37

Yelling Kids

A man rides through a crowd, a king in regular clothes. His heart bursting as he hears the cries of the crowd, 'God help us. God help us.' For a few moments the masses have forgotten the pressures and fears and terrors of their lives, set aside the things which steer their every move. For now they see a man on a donkey and they believe everything will be all right. And so they cheer. And he sees the smiles, hears the cheers and the children's laughter, senses the resurrected hope in the air. Some watch and wonder, trying to second-guess whether this is their moment, whether this long-predicted happening will fit their plans. But it's beyond their control. Too humble, too gentle, too visibly saturated in integrity and kindness.

And as he nears the temple a hush falls, and the crowd hold their breath. And as the first tables turn and the currencies of dominance and control tumble to the floor, it seems as if this might be the time for ousting the power-brokers, the exclusive warriors who rule with pride and arrogance. But the dust settles, and instead of sword thrusts and bloodshed there is the sound of children running wild, gushing around the place like living water. Spurred on by the breath of the spirit as it blows suddenly through the temple. The son of David's in town and the kids are yelling about it. Irrepressible. And then there is the sound of stumbling footsteps as sick people, the poor and the cautious, come limping in to draw hope from his smiling grace. For a moment here the walls have fallen, and the den of thieves has become a place to freely encounter God once more.

Matthew 21

Disappointed

He's tired. Wraps his hands around his face, rubs at the frown lines and the rings under his eyes. It wasn't supposed to be this way. Three years ago, when he was bored, something happened. Life broke into his dull existence. Freedom rose like the new sun. Promises were passed around. Then somewhere along the way, the narrative changed. And the boredom crept back. Now he wakes each morning wondering when? When exactly will things change? Why are they still traipsing through villages and down back streets, mixing it with women and children, strays and losers? Why does the talk continue while the clouds still hang over them? They may tell tales of freedom but no one's free. And the hero refuses to rise. Every chance to fight back and the carpenter somehow steps aside, leans towards peace.

He's beginning to think he has to do something. Take a risk. Make something happen. They'll call him a traitor. A rebel in the worst sense. But perhaps this was the plan all along. Perhaps that's why he was chosen. Maybe they're all just waiting for him to do his job. Bring on the bad guys and set the scene for the showdown. So the revolution can really begin. So the talking can cease, and the battle begin. And it'll be over in a blink anyway. With his power the carpenter'll soon oust the invaders. With a clap of his hands the oppressors will be clutching at their chests, feeling their hearts give out. There might even be angels and a host of heavenly warriors. So it's just a matter of time and place. He stands up, paces, adjust the strap of the money bag on his shoulder. Money. That'll do it. He'll go to the authorities, offer to set up an ambush for them, do it for 30 pieces of silver. But really, he'll be a double agent. Doing the dirty work. Bringing the chance they're all waiting for. It won't be betrayal at all. It'll be victory. At last. What could go wrong?

Matthew 26 vv 14–16

Inside Man

A man in charge barely contains his fury. He's had a bellyful of this. He snarls at the others and they growl back, but no one has any real answers. How often must he belittle them?

How often must he make them look foolish in public? He's just one man for goodness sake. How hard can it be to bring him down? They've apprehended fools and rebels before, dangerous men who would so easily bring the might of Rome down on them all. Just a whisper of revolution and they all know what that means. A nervous governor calling in the troops to start burning the temple. No. They cannot have that. And he cannot continue to weave his reckless way, talking of freedom and a new way. What they need is a man on the inside. Someone who'll set up an ambush for them, someone who can lead them to a quiet place away from the crowds and the adoring fans. Someone who might just do it for a fistful of silver…

John 11 vv 45–52

The Message

Two men look a little lost, they mumble something repeatedly as if trying not to forget. A secret message of some kind. One of them stops, snaps his fingers and points ahead. A man carrying a pitcher of water stops and frowns. He eyes up the two men approaching him. They look tense, as if they are worried about being found out.

They hover in front of him, as if one is waiting for the other to speak. They exchange furtive glances. The man with the pitcher shifts his feet. The pitcher's heavy, come on, if you've got something to say, say it.

One of them manages to mutter, 'The teacher says it's…'

He falters, trying to remember the right phrase. So the other one jumps in.

'…time,' the second one finishes for him. 'It's his time, Where's the guest room…'

'...the one for the Passover meal,' the other says.

The man nods. That's close enough. The message he's been told to wait for. The secret signal he was expecting so the teacher can enjoy his Passover in safety. Away from the crowds and the threats from the High Priest. He says nothing, nods, and leads the way. They follow him up the narrow stairs to a room they've never seen before. By some miracle the place has been arranged for them perfectly. They start setting things up...

Luke 22 vv 7–13

Friends

Abraham saw a new day, a day that would blow the minds of those who would hear of it and then tell it to others. About a God who stops child sacrifice, offering blessing instead. Removing the curse of superstition and fear. The message had come down the line to Abraham, take your son, your only son and sacrifice him. And if Abraham's heart shattered into a thousand pieces that day, he didn't show it. Instead he got things together and prepared to lay the life of his long-awaited and cherished son on the line, because that's what you did. To please the gods back then you gave your children. For better weather, for better crops, and fingers crossed the gods won't punish you. So the two saddle up and hike off into the dawn. And yet the outcome was not as expected. Stop Abraham. Stop! Lay down the knife. Free the boy. Here, have this ram instead. No child sacrifice, not today. In fact, not anymore. Not ever. Not for this true God. Instead another kind of offering hung in the air. One which involved listening and understanding and following in the creator's footsteps. Unthinkable in those days. A discovery about the living God which blew everything out of the water. Rewrote the rule book. A God you could trust, a relationship which had the potential to grow. Perhaps somehow old Abraham knew that his God wanted another kind of sacrifice. Wait here, he had said to his servants, we're off to worship and then *we'll come back*. Both of us. Somehow he saw a miracle beforehand. Because they did come back. Both man and boy. And that kyboshed child sacrifice for good.

And now a group of disciples sit around looking a little awkward. Frowning at their feet. They're being offered another step closer to the Almighty. Something they can't quite grasp. Friendship. With God. Really? And not just any god. The one who is above everything else. All wise, all powerful, all present. It's unthinkable. Friendship. With God! Not fearful slavery, in which you could be misused and thrown aside, but a committed, trusting agreement. Their minds are spinning as the carpenter talks. Using words they never expected. Can this be true? Does he mean what they think he means? Abraham saw a day in which his son Isaac was resurrected, and a ram's life laid down. Now even animal sacrifice is on the line. Because friendship with God will spring from love touching the earth, sealed with gentle, courageous surrender and a tomb-busting son-rise. Justice and peace kissing, love and truth embracing. Righteousness smiling down from heaven, and salvation filling the land. What was the promise Abraham heard? I will bless every family on earth through you. Well here it comes. The fulfilment of that. Every family blessed, as this carpenter says to them, I don't call you my servants anymore, I call you my friends.

Genesis 22, Psalm 85 vv 9–11, John 15 v 15

Part 10:
Fully Human

Questions of Life

Did your weary feet ache from the steps you took?

Did you sometimes sit quietly doing nothing but look?

Did you ever sneeze from the dust and the dirt?

Did you ever laugh so much and so hard that it hurt?

Did you do so much good that wasn't on show?

Did you meet more people than we'll ever know?

Did you dance at those parties and stay till the end?

Did you cry at the funerals of family and friends?

Did you love the wide smiles at the tales you told?

Did you love to see people come in from the cold?

Did you glimpse new horizons in the listeners' eyes?

Did you welcome the questions, the when, where and whys?

Did you rehearse your parables out there on your own?

Did you act them out as you brought them home?

Did you enjoy all that food you shared all the time?

And just how often did you turn water to wine?

Did you have favourite food as you walked along?

Did you have a favourite feelgood song?

Did you have your own go-to happy place?

Did you miss your childhood, and those old school days?

Did you have bags under your eyes from sleepless nights?
Did you ever relax, did you feel uptight?
Did your heart sink at times at the size of the crowd?
Did you think about looking for the quickest way out?

Did you ever get emotional, did your heart skip a beat?
Did you lie in some days, did you doze in the heat?
Did you ever do a double-take, and if so why?
Did a view leave you breathless, with a heartfelt sigh?

Did you ever get bored, in your carpentry days?
Did you ever arm-wrestle with Peter and James?
Did you imagine our life now, with its cell phones and cars?
Did you see skateboards and YouTube and rockets to Mars?

Does it bother you when we forget you lived life?
That you well understand our trouble and strife?
Do you want to gatecrash our meetings sometimes?
Do you wander in secretly and sit there in disguise?

Will heaven just be about singing and prayers?
Or will there be maths, parties, and musical chairs?
Will there be gardening and sport, art and debates?
And science, and feasts, and a three-legged race?

Will clocks be banned so we'll never be late?
Will we eat what we choose and not put on weight?
Will we live in the moment, in the now, and the here?
With no past regrets, and no future to fear?

Part 11:
Adventures in Emptiness

Why?

'Why should I let my son wander the earth and make his way towards a murderous crossbeam? For the life of a rejected woman? For the life of a whole universe? For the rebirth of the cosmos? For the second chance of a brutal criminal? For every small or great, known or unknown crime or misdemeanour? For the author of this book? For the reader of this book…?

Or perhaps, for all of them?'

Abandonment

'And will it make his abandonment by me that much harder because my dear beloved son is convinced that everyone else might leave him but I, his father, never would. And will knowing that make it so much harder for me too? *The time is coming, he told his friends, when you will all leave me. But I am not alone, because the father is with me.* And yet, I will let go of his hand, I will vacate his heart and mind and will and strength. Not because I want to, oh no, but because I must choose that way. The way of emptiness. So that the way of fullness will rise once more, and so that no one ever has to feel that abandoned again.'

Wi-Fi

I try and remind myself frequently that Jesus stepped into reality. His life was hard. He grew up in a poor neighbourhood. His background was questionable in human terms. Who *was* his real father? (A question which may have been frequently thrown at him.) Taxes were high, he lived in an occupied country. He started work at a young age, and he had at least four brothers and two sisters. So he knew well the rigours of family life. At some point he lost his dad. And when he finally began his three-year tenure as the rescuer everyone was longing for, he was misunderstood, insulted, rejected, threatened, ignored, belittled, and eventually beaten and murdered. He faced conflict every day. These days we might have worried about his mental health. Jesus was not superman. He needed food and drink to survive. He needed to sleep and go to the loo. And time alone with his God was a life-saver for him. In Hosea chapter 2 v 14, the prophet tells of God wooing his people into the wilderness so he can speak tenderly to them. I reckon that's why Jesus regularly sought out those empty wilderness places, places without first century Wi-Fi, so he could hear the tender voice of his father once more. It kept him sane. Kept him alive. Kept him focussed and nourished. 'I have food you know nothing about,' he told his friends on several occasions. The food of time with his Creator-dad fed his strained, hungry and battered soul. He certainly knew what it was to hunger and thirst for righteousness. He worked for it every day, laid down his life for it every day. It must have been exhausting. And as well as needing the kind of sleep and meals we all need, he fed on Isaiah 55's banquet. It kept him going, kept him on the road to a garden of grief and a hill of death.

Paradox

How can we ever start to know the inner thoughts and feelings of the fully human fully divine son of God. All that he carried for those three years, all that he carried for 33 years. Zoom in on Ephesians chapter 3 v 19 and you'll notice we are told that we cannot understand fully the extent and nature of the love of God – 'May you experience the love of Jesus, though it is too great to understand fully…' A conundrum really. A riddle slow-cooked in an enigma and sautéed in a paradox. And I wonder whether this is also true for the apprehension, stress, passion, wonder, laughter, patience, compassion, longings of Jesus. All of these things too great for us to fully understand. One thing is for sure though, if he was fully human, then he experienced all that we experience. Or to quote from those liberating lines in Hebrews 4 v 15 – 'This High Priest of ours understands our weaknesses, for he faced all of the same temptations we do, yet he did not sin.'

Crumbling

And so, with all this in mind, aware of my narrow vision, and blurred outlook, I take up my laptop in the year of grace 2022, and go back to the time when a man wrestled with the world, and himself, and his father. The genuine, understanding, compassionate one who set the world turning, and knew what it was to wash feet and hold filthy hands. Having spent so many days in the light, bringing others into the light, he now willingly steps into the dark. Having built so many friendships and connections, he now chooses isolation and loneliness. Having established a flawless universe, he has walked its paths and knows so well the lost souls and longing hearts, too many spiritual zombies forever jostling under restless skies, enslaved by the crumbling rooftops of their fragile lives. That is why he has come, to put the light back into their eyes. And that is why he is here now. In this garden. Ready to wrestle with the forces of darkness. Darkness which bled into this world in a whole other garden. Let's turn the clock back further for a moment…

Eve & Adam

A man wakes to another day, but this one features a whole new thing, a sense of something never seen, tasted, smelt or felt before. There have been many new things lately. But this is a morning of *if only*. A sensation never felt by anyone before. An ache, a longing to rearrange the pieces, change the picture, make it all right again. He can still see the footprints in the dirt, the path that led to a planet shift. He plays the events in his mind, again and again. Maybe somehow they will lead to a different place if he goes over them enough times. Like watching a film with a sad end replayed enough times to make it turn out happy. And the sad fact is it could have been so easily avoided. If only, if only if only. How many times will that refrain haunt the atmosphere in the ages to come. He follows the scuffed footprints. Four of them in a row, slightly out of step. The day is warming up, the birds fill the soundscape with their song. Maybe it's okay after all. Maybe he was overthinking it. Maybe the future will be bright and untainted. She's standing there looking up. Right at that place where the fruit used to be. That thing which seemed so appetising last night.

That thing which will define everything now. Not merely that extra box of chocolates you downed, or that inadvisable film you watched, or those short sharp words you sprayed at the person you love. (Just because a person you did not love and barely know, hurt you earlier in the day.) No, those things can matter of course. But this thing matters much more than those. This thing will matter to the world entire. This thing is a tuneless song that will play like white noise in the lives of everyone that is ever to come. This thing will be the very reason for stuffing in too many chocolates or lashing out in anger or disrespect. This will be the cause of every last moment of fallout to come. And that is why we must jump to a meal which celebrates slaves being set free…

Eating

I don't know how he ate anything at that Passover supper. While others shovelled down the precious delights of that freedom meal and guzzled those plentiful glasses of meaningful wine. Did he watch and nibble on a few bits? Well aware of what the night ahead held for him. Knowing that he would surely bring back anything he had half-digested. Knowing he would not get the benefit of the feast he was sharing with his oblivious friends. They of course would get the benefit. They and the aeons of generations that would put their faltering feet in the dusty prints of those first friends. This meal will last forever. The bread will never go stale, this wine never turn to vinegar. Look at all my trials and tribulations, the disciples would one day sing in a musical version of this epic. A weariness washes suddenly over him, a wave of despair breaking across his heart. A thought crosses his mind and he says it out loud.

'I sent you out before without a backup plan, on the kind of mission which flourished when you relied upon me. But tonight we're hovering on the verge of another mission, and you'll lose sight of me for a while. I must face the troubles ahead defenceless and vulnerable. So you should prepare yourselves. Steel yourselves and stock up. There's a battle ahead so be warned and arm yourselves.'

He knows some of them will be anticipating a showdown with the authorities, a chance to rise up and take control. Two of them hold up blades. He flinches a little. Quickly closes the conversation down. His mind is awash with a million thoughts. Has he prepared them enough? He knows they will struggle, and he knows he must be prepared later. Tonight more than ever the way of surrender must prevail. His friends will see it another way, and at least one of them will resort to violence. So he'll be ready for the fight, for the lashing out in the confusion. The mob may come for him with swords and clubs, but he will come with healing in his hands.

Panic

On the night Jesus was arrested everyone was in panic. An opportunity had arisen out of the blue, Judas went pounding through the night, his footsteps a call of betrayal that would echo down the centuries, but no one was ready. Not the disciples, not the priests, not the soldiers, and certainly not Pilate. Only one person knew what was going on and what was to come. And he was in the garden kneeling alone, blood on his brow, prayers on his lips, eternity in his heart. And he was willing to stay there all night if needs be, waiting for the rest of the clowns to get their act together. He certainly waited a couple of hours, long enough for his friends to doze off a couple of times. Judas bangs on someone's door, rattles the nerves of the High Priest with his sudden claims. Jesus is no longer surrounded by supportive crowds, there are only shadows on his shoulders now, and a few friends who'll most likely run scared when they see the enemy rising like a blood moon. Now's your chance. Wake up. Get things organised. This chance may not come again. And so there is hurrying, and panic, and pulling robes, and tripping over feet, and blundering and cussing. And the irony is none of that was necessary. Jesus was in no hurry. Waiting for the will of his father was something he'd rehearsed all his life. Certainly the last three years of it anyway, the rest is a bit of a mystery. Those who claimed to be in control were not, the one who looked as if he had failed completely… he was the one who knew exactly what was happening. He was the only one with his finger on the pulse as chaos raged around him… or to reimagine the events of that night another way…

Part 12:
Night Falls

Now!

A man runs, flees, deep into the night, fleeing his past, his hopes, his motives, his disappointment. Like a drug addict staring at his needle and kidding himself he will fix things tomorrow, he looks at himself as he flees, knowing that this may not go well, but unable somehow to resist. Behind him he leaves a trail of theories, future debates and arguments about why, why he is doing this, what went wrong. Money? Power? Criminality? Fake discipleship? Misunderstanding? Trying to force a Messiah's hand? Who knows... maybe a little of all these things. Ahead of him, around a corner he cannot see, lies a noose. A future he never planned. He catches his breath, steadies himself against the wall as he pauses in the archway of the High Priest's house. The gatekeeper nods knowingly, steps by to let him pass. He hides his face a little as he slopes through. No one is ready for him. Oh they all schemed about this night coming. Wove their lurid webs and talked of revenge for the arguments they lost and the misguided fools they have appeared to be in public. But they never imagined this, the hired accomplice staggering in now, spilling his guts, fear and fire in his eyes as he spews the words that will determine this planet's future.

'Now!' he barks. 'It's now! What are you sitting there for? Get up! Get up!'

Caiaphas is about to blast him, burn him off for this disrespectful intrusion. Then he hesitates, thinks again.

'You mean…'

'Yes! Gethsemane.' He gestures behind him, spit cascading in flecks as he yelps the words. 'He's alone. Praying. No crowds. Just a few of his cronies… well you know… his friends. You know.'

Caiaphas pushes him out of the way, a discarded serf he no longer has any purpose for. He snaps his fingers and the others leap up too. But no one is really ready. Not yet.

Pilate

'Hurry!' The High Priest snaps. 'Or he'll get away. Cheat us again. Slip away once more. Up!! NOW!!'

Orders are issued for the getting of temple guards, soldiers well-versed in beatings and belittlings. An underling battles his way through the bodies and out the door.

'Pilate!' someone gasps, and everyone stops their scrambling again.

'Pilate?' says Caiaphas.

'Yes. If this is to be the end… you know, the real end… we need the Governor's say-so to finish him. And he'll not do it without warning. Not now. Not so late. We need to request an audience.'

'But we don't have time! Not for this! Not now! He'll get away!'

'We have to make time.'

Spatters

And back there in the garden, spatters of sweat and blood decorating the ground around his knees, the son of man

144

prays. Very aware of his humanity now. Fully human, fully alive. Every cell of his body charged with fear. The words stutter from his mouth. Prayers so honest, so true that only the son of man could have prayed them. He pours it all out, a torrent of reality to his father. Thank God for his father, here with him, while everyone else sleeps or schemes against him. A figure draws near. One he recognises from those days in the desert. And boy, does this feel like a desert now. And so here's that angel, the one who calmed the wild animals, now come to calm the beasts raging in the spiritual realm, the furious creatures intent on terrifying him, not to death, but back towards life. Away from the death that could make everything live again. The demons hiss and urge him to choose another way. A road just a fragment wider. Who'd notice anyway if he gave his life another night, in another way? Who'd mind if he slipped away quietly in his sleep? Who'd worry if he fell under a passing chariot? Something quicker, something less public. Behind him, back there in the garden his friends had worried at first, tried to coax one another into going to ask the question. Is he all right? He looks troubled, more stressed than they've ever seen before. You go. No you go. But he's praying, wouldn't want to disturb him. Disturb? He looks well disturbed all ready. And so one or two make moves, take a step or two, eventually melting back into the darkness, overwhelmed by a greater sense of something coming. Something larger than this world. Something they fear will overpower them all. Better to leave him to battle it alone.

Life and Death

And so the messengers run. And stand at the gate. Struggling to articulate their message to the pagan invaders

145

as they battle to catch their breath. Will the Roman Governor please see us? Yes tonight. No it can't wait. Yes he will want to dispense with this matter. No this is no mere awkward religious argument. Yes it's a matter of life and death. No we're not joking. The soldiers roll their eyes in their shiny pagan helmets. One of them turns and disappears, the other stares at the messengers and sneers.

Warriors and Snoring

He feels the heartening pressure of angelic fingers on his shoulder. Strengthening, calming. The presence of invisible warriors. Rooting for him. On his side. He stands and walks back to his friends. How long have they been here now? Hours certainly. So long that weary men had fallen asleep. They didn't know this was coming when they ate so well and drank so much. Now look at them. Dead to the world. Dreaming of better things no doubt. Certainly not imagining what will come this way all too soon. He shakes an arm, jabs at a foot with his sandal. Urges them to pray for him. They sit up, mutter something incomprehensible, wipe spit from their chins, wonder how much longer this night will go on. Can they not just go back to Bethany and sleep in comfort there? Wake up to Martha's breakfast and a peaceful sunrise? Please? But he's moved away again. This night will go on. Here. For who knows how long. In this place of lonely darkness. This place of crawling gloom and grim shadows. It might be hours yet before the fools in power get their act together. But he will wait. Every second, every minute. On and on and on. Because a world is waiting. And this is the place to be. He hears a series of thuds as the bodies of his friends collapse back down again. Not so much wrestling in prayer as slipping into oblivion once more. There is the sound of snoring as he lifts his head and pours out his troubles again.

Devious

Judas wanders now. Suddenly alone. Suddenly foolish. Around him priests and armed men run this way and that. Every so often shouldering him out of the way. He doesn't understand why he is suddenly sidelined. Useless. A sub on the bench when he was expecting to score the winning goal. He paces in a straggling line, doing his best to avoid them. Before he knows it the place empties. Just a couple of servant girls near the courtyard fire.

'Aren't you going with them then?' says one, more confident than he ever expected.

He looks at the open gateway. A head reappears, one of the priests sent by Caiaphas no doubt. No words, just a gesturing finger, beckoning him, reeling him in. Maybe he'll still be useful after all. And as he follows he remembers. That sign he promised to make. That aberration of friendship. That deviant call sign he'd suggested. It had seemed clever a few hours back. Devious perhaps. Now it makes him feel a little sick.

Glimpses

Every minute is an hour. The gloom lurks like a waiting predator. He longs for the chance to live again, a way to re-tread the tracks of these last three years. Faces pass before him, the moments of amazement, the bursts of laughter, 12 baskets exploding with fish and bread, a river of wine at a Cana wedding. Children giggling and running to hug him, sick and injured rejects standing tall and dancing unhindered in the street. Rejected women finding their feet and their voices and their dignity once more. So much life, so many glimpses of resurrection. He wants it all back, pounds his brain for a solution, runs down the corridors of his mind looking for a way out. Another plan, a different redemptive plot once hatched before the dawn of the world, forgotten and tucked away in a dusty corner. Some other way. A road without thorns and nails and fists. Surely there must be… surely there must be… surely there must be…

Twisted

At last the twisted scheme is set in place, soldiers, priests and hangers-on gather in the flickering torchlight, faces scarred with intent. And so they walk, Judas at the back, wondering now, what has he started? Couldn't someone else have played his part? Wasn't this a role for someone worse than him? Someone truly depraved? Will this be what he is remembered for? Perhaps it's still okay though. Perhaps the son of man will rise as the son of David, leap on a white horse and fell these fools with one slice of his sword. It's possible. It could all end differently. He may still have been part of a revolution. He may still be a keystone in a salvation story.

He is of course. Though he doesn't know it.

Cup

The snoring goes on, and something about the rhythm is calming, and he senses strength coursing through his veins now. Courage rising in his DNA. Some deep purpose welling up from the dawn of time. His prayers have slowed, and the words have begun to change. The will of his father has become his focus. He wants another cup to drink, of course he does, with every ounce of himself, and yet and yet... he does not want to sup a concoction of his own making. His own will. It's his father's purpose. That is why he's here. That's always been the reason. That is why he has waited in the dark for so long.

Little

Pilate is a little man. In stature anyway. And his mind is not as large as he likes to think. When he comes out though the messengers still lose height a little. Not so much bowing as shrinking. They gabble their request and the Roman sighs. Footsteps. His wife appears. Now she's the sharp one. Her eyes take in everything. Her ears too. The exchange rattles on. She doesn't like it. All this talk of false prophets and insurrection. Of temples being torn down and one man sinking the empire. Really? I mean... really? She sighs too. Narrows her eyes. They exchange glances. Pilate paces. She waits. It's only when the two messengers have backed off, turned and scurried away, that she speaks.

'You're taking this seriously?'

'Don't start. You know as well as I do these people take their Messiahs seriously. It's the wrong time to turn them down. Too many pilgrims in town. We need to keep the peace.'

'But at this time of night?

'The sooner the better. We settle the dispute and dispense with the rebel. Or rather I settle this dispute and I dispense with the rebel. You go to bed.'

She shakes her head and turns away; she knows what she's like. She's bound to dream about all this now.

Kiss

The messengers have to run now. The mob have gone, set off, gone for Gethsemane. They need to catch up, or they'll miss the show. The action.

A kiss in the dark. Normally associated with warmth and romance, now tagged with betrayal and tragedy. Now it signals a friendship lost and a back turned. And even as he embraces Judas, he sees, over his friend's shoulder, the mass of them, the seething mob. They've brought an ocean when a stream would have been enough. He won't fight, of course he won't, he's been waiting here with his father, waiting for this very moment, why else would he stay so long in this grim garden? Judas steps back and to the side, and a line of thugs moves in, but not before he moves towards them, and for some reason they fear an attack, fear that he has legions of angels ready to wipe them out. So they falter and stagger back a little, as if he's slaughtered them with nothing more than a smile. So he waits for them to regroup, and while he does that his best mate lurches. There's a flash of metal, a yelp and a fountain of red in the torchlight. 'No!' his voice cuts through everything, full of command and control. He places a firm hand on Peter's arm, forces him to lower the blood-smeared blade. And he cups the wound on the injured man's face, catches the blood in his palm as he presses against it. And the pained expression melts into confusion. Suddenly there is no pain, no crimson leakage. The servant stares wide-eyed. For a moment it is as if the miracle has sorted everything and the garden falls silent. Not for long though. 'Live by the sword and you'll die by it Peter,' he says. And that seems to be a signal for those who do want to live by it. More weapons flash, hands grab, ropes are lashed and he's led away. And all his friends, some of them still rubbing sleep from their eyes, watch in a kind of bleary terror, wondering just what happened. Till two of the soldiers wave a spear and then they leap out of the way, turn and kick up dust as they go. Some of them not stopping until the safety of Bethany is within sight once more. And somewhere in their heads lean promises of fighting and protecting and self-sacrifice ring hollow in their minds.

Running

But not Peter, even as he wipes his sword and shoves it back through his belt once more he is off. Determined to make good on his vow. Run? Never. Deny? You're kidding right. And as he moves after the mob another figure steps from the darkness. Judas, his lips still damp from the disloyal kiss, finds another role. If Peter wants to follow to the bitter end, then only one disciple can get him into the High Priest's courtyard. Only one disciple has become a familiar face there. Judas will show him the way. Perhaps his finest hour has come. Behind them in the shadows two more disciples wait. One, a young teenager, disturbed from his bed, makes to follow the other two, but it's not long before a stray soldier spots him, grabs his protective blanket and watches guffawing as the boy panics and scarpers, wrapped in nothing more than his fear. Never mind. One day the boy will retell this tale, along with so many other stories. And his account will echo down the centuries, changing lives along the way. The other lone figure is a young fisherman who digs deep and finds an ounce of courage. But he'll not be so public as Peter, he'll wait, and dodge from shadow to shadow, till eventually he will stand in the longest shadow of all. The cross that will shed its image down the centuries and into forever.

Silent

And so the garden falls silent. Gethsemane. The place of epic conflict, this no-man's land of wrestling with God, on this night when winning the war actually means losing the battle.

Part 13:
Enthroned

Flashback – 40 Days

Long before all this, just after his watery commission, when his cousin and his father presented him to the crowds, he took a walk. Knew he had to do it. And the walk became a dry adventure. A wilderness walkabout. And as he trudged through that wilderness, in those 40 days of space and silence and emptiness, with time on his hands and the thoughts and questions rattling like stones in his mind...

Did he see the struggles others would face?

Did he feel the pain of loss and loneliness?

Did he sense the wrestling of more than flesh and blood?

Did he glimpse the wars and wounds that would rage?

Did he know the rejection and ridicule of worldly ignorance?

And did those times of temptation prepare him for the most crucial temptation of all, in that garden of blood and sweat and prayer, when his dry-lipped words would change from, 'Father take this cup from me.' to 'Your will be done.'

40 days to prepare himself, to change shape, to become the servant king, unafraid of washing feet and embracing the unloved.

40 days to sharpen his vision and see so clearly that power and pride and manipulation were not the way to change things.

40 days to tune into the ever-present tender voice of the One who loved him, and valued him, the source and calling and destiny of his being and doing.

40 days for history. 40 days that would last forever.

Every Crime

As he hangs enthroned now, the king of all kings, the humble leader of all humble leaders, the victim of all victims, the scorned of all those scorned... does he see every crime, every assault, ever split-second of abuse, every pain, every hurt, every embarrassment, every injustice, every fumbled line, every misguided step, every selfish inclination, every miry thought... as he hangs on the cross. In those turbulent, endless hours. Does he feel every jolt, suffer every wound, taste the salt from every tear... there is little doubt something is happening, because thousands have hung on crosses before, and yet not changed the world, not enveloped the broken and injured ages of history. Does he see the faces of the millions, the seething mass, each precious figure, shaped and rendered by him before time began. Hear the questions and cries and clashes. Smell the fear and the blood and the sweat. Sense the loss. So much loss. Bear a burden beyond bearing. All the whys and rejections and horrors coursing through his being, a billion starving rats gouging pieces from him with every scuttling step.

Kangaroo

There's a kangaroo court before all this though. No hope of an honest verdict, too much water under the bridge and too much litter in that water. The future is sealed. Just a case of making it appear somehow legal. Witnesses prattle and hurl nonsensical accusations. Power players think they know what's going on, kid themselves that they are in control of all this. A puppet king gets an audience with the prisoner, though no good comes of it. He's wanted to wipe out this Nazareth man for a while, but for now he just gets to mock and taunt this stranger. He appears to have a whole other idea about kingship and rule, Herod wonders why he ever felt so threatened. This wandering teacher's just a dishevelled peasant, doesn't have the first idea about wealth and power. So unimpressed, he sends the prisoner away again, dismisses him with a sulky flap of his hand, and the nervous Roman governor finds himself grabbed by the scruff and forced to adjudicate. The governor's wife, who seems to know more about what's going on than he does, talks of nightmares and an innocent man. Pilate rubs his face, hard, doing his best to wipe the stress from his mind. Agh people! What are they like! Why can't he have an easy life? He asks the prisoner if he sees himself as a king, and the prisoner deftly hands the responsibility back to the governor. The prisoner won't say much, but what he says makes him all the surer his wife is onto something here. Why does he sense that this weakened, blood-soaked man is somehow the one in control here? How can that be? And what good will come of another execution? The crowd chant and Pilate's plan goes wrong. Do they really choose to free a twisted rebel in favour of killing this king? Why not free this humble king? The chanting goes on and it's fuelled with threats now. He's in a corner and he knows nothing can be done. So if nothing else, he commissions a sign for the cross. A message to the world. No he won't change it. He's made his mind up, you've got your criminal, now murder him. And fix that sign above him. *The king of the Jews.*

The End of Everything?

A man stands and stares, unblinking for a while, though eventually a microscopic splinter from the wood settles on his cornea and he has to shut his eye and rub it. Or is that for some other reason? He has good eyesight, has always had excellent vision, but he's never seen so clearly as he does today. He cannot know what is going on under the surface, who ever could? But he sees the body, shifting and twitching and flinching, like a thousand others before, and he hears the gasps and cries. Yet this is not the same. Not at all.

He has heard the rumours, and there have been many. People pass by as he stands stock still, blocking his eyeline for a moment, shadows and ghosts compared to the vibrancy of the figure in his line of sight. Strange. He's staring at a dying man and yet it's everyone else who seems less alive, all these passing strangers. These lost souls talking, yawning, drinking, leering, wandering back and forth, kicking at stones. There are tears and taunts and troubles poured out. Life goes on. And yet something about the man on the hill has jammed a stick in the restless clock of the ages. And now for some reason he finds his mind wandering back to a conversation he had with another officer.

A strange tale of a servant falling sick. A strange tale of a servant regaining strength. Perhaps he should have taken more notice of the story. He can't grasp the details right now, and yet something tells him there is a connection between that day and this one. He finds himself wondering what will happen when the dying is done. When the cross has finished its work and the suffering subsides. Will something extraordinary happen? And if it does will it only be him who notices?

Right now the prisoner is clearly in hell, plundering the depths of despair, his frame labouring and taut as if he is working hard, mining another world for condemned souls. And now he's straining to turn his head, lips moving in response to the prisoner beside him. Another man dying in agony. There are in fact three men up there yet the one in the middle is different. Something is going on here. Something that smacks of eternity. This is not in vain. Not just another case of conviction, ridicule, torture and killing. Oh yes, there are the usual nails involved but something else is keeping the victim in place. And there's a weight on this man, a responsibility, and one that somehow he's bearing well. As if he's carrying the torment and the loneliness of the whole world. Not merely another Atlas condemned to hold up the heavens, but a man choosing to bring heaven down here. A man? Or more?

The officer knows all about gods. There are plenty of them. Jupiter, Mars, Minerva, Neptune, Saturn, Venus... gods of war, time, love, wisdom, the seas and skies... and yet has any of them achieved the heights of this man? They all seem a little futile in this moment here, a little impotent. Why is he thinking like this? Where are these wonderings coming from? Why is his mind veering into that territory? Is he going mad, thinking of Jupiter and Mars in the same breath as a convicted criminal? Yet still the questions race on, chasing each other around the arena of his mind like a pack of rabid wolves. What's happening to him? He thought he'd been forever hardened by too many nailings. Thought his heart had been coffin-sealed long ago. Was sure he'd seen it all and more.

He thinks of his wife, her anxious face sneaking across his mind, the marriage not what it once was. And his twins, just turned four, all innocence and curiosity and wonder. He's glad they're not here for this day's work. He's glad they're not here for any of his days' work, his life sectioned off, split between the family man and the efficient leader. The caring father on one hand, the man who goes killing for a living on the other.

There's a thunderclap overhead and the ground groans and shifts a little. The weather is changing, spoiling for a fight, the clouds broiling and moshing up there. Are they disturbed by this too? Has the stench of innocent sweat and blood set them spoiling for a fight? Is this the end of everything? Or just the start?

He looks back at that man. The one who is somehow the centre of the universe right now. One of the other criminals is spitting and coughing his last. The other is oddly calm up there. And in the middle Jesus raises his head and releases a cry from the core of his being. One of desperation and loneliness. He lifts his face higher, flicks his head from side to side, side to side, side to side, as if searching desperately for a sign. And then eventually, his last energy spent, he stares straight ahead, his face gaunt, the cheeks bruised and hollow, and he whispers something. Then he bows his head and surrenders himself.

And the officer speaks. Not something he'd planned to say. Not something he ever imagined saying. Not something he yet understands. But the words are there on his lips all the same. Sure and solid as a rock.

'This man was the son of God.'

Wilderness Voice

A voice calls out in the wilderness,
In the wild spaces,
In the depths of silence and groaning,
In the places of aching loneliness.
A voice calls out,
Offering comfort and a way forward.
'Lift up your eyes, look to the skies,
And to the one who set them in place.
Bring your troubles to him,
Your anxieties, your fears about the future,
The burdens that wear you down,
The fog that blurs your vision,
And the despair that steals your hope.
Bring your troubles and all that is on your mind,
Bring your emptiness and your loss.
Bring those things which make your heart ache,
Those things which haunt your soul.
Bring the panic and the racing thoughts,
Pour them out, as if talking with a friend.
Bring them each day and each night.
They are too much for you to carry alone.
So come as you are, wherever you are,
With your mess and your muddle,
Your fears, your fury and your frustration.
Please come, the real you, that is enough.'

Part 14:

Saturday

Waiting

A day of waiting, when waiting actually feels like an end.

In Bethany men and women stir and wake, though waking feels like the worst thing they could do right now. Some walk and look.

Out.

Over creation.

As God looked and saw that it was good.

But they see desolation.

Emptiness.

The loss of a vision.

Three years down the drain.

Wasted.

So much seemed different about Jesus.

So much seemed possible.

But now he has gone the way of all the other so-called Messiahs.

Overpowered by the pagan invaders.

If Jesus couldn't stand up to the might of Rome, who can?

Questions hang in the air, unspoken.

What now?

Why did we run?

Couldn't we have saved him?

What was he expecting of us?

Did the big fisherman really cry so hard?

And was that Judas in the dark with his lips puckered?

Betrayal all over him like spatters of slurry?

All those stories the carpenter told, all those profound sayings and comments, they now seem empty, impotent.

Yet here's Lazarus, once so deathly sick and yet alive now, walking about, standing silently with them, breathing, the colour in his cheeks as he chews on his lip.

If Lazarus can be all right, why can't Jesus?

Martha's busy, of course she is, best way to avoid all these questions. She burst her heart when her brother died, she can't bear to let out that kind of pain again, not so soon.

And Mary, she sits in the dirt, gripping handfuls of dust, throwing them in the air so the grit settles on her cheeks. Silent grief etched on her face and forehead. So many lines.

Thomas is the only one talking, blustering, thinking as he speaks. It's his way. Eventually he wanders off on his own, so he can rant to himself, avoiding the critical stares of the others. He can't stand the silence. And he can't escape the words that slipped from his lips not so long ago. *Let's go to Jerusalem with Jesus and die there with him.* He said that, just as Jesus was setting off to come and pull Lazarus from the jaws of death. A claim which sounds so hollow now.

'I'm going away and you know where I'm going...' Tom recalls the words that had mystified him at the Passover meal. Where was he intending to go? Back to Nazareth? Was that his plan, to escape before the priests came and took him? Where else could he have been going? He had talked about his father. Something about the way. Maybe it was Nazareth. Joseph had long-since died. Maybe that was it! Joseph had died and Jesus was going to join him. Really? Was that a plan? It didn't sound like one, not from the man who had talked of holding life in all its fullness. Where was his revolution now? None of this made sense.

And for a moment there an image flashes into his mind, an appalling vision of the carpenter's hand and a jagged hole right through it where a nail had once been.

Bits and Pieces

Imagine this. A beloved and despised carpenter from Nazareth is taken down from a cross on which he has died, and he is laid in another man's tomb, late on a Friday afternoon. And then early on the following Sunday morning, as dawn is on the verge of breaking, he wakes, and breathes and lives again, resurrected by his father in heaven. And then he stops time. Because he has things to do before his friends come to the tomb. He sneaks over to my house and walks through the door, because he can do that now, and he can see all the broken bits and pieces of my life. The mistakes, and regrets, and questions, and doubts, and weaknesses, and trip-ups, and face-plants. He can see them all there, strewn across the carpet. And he gathers them up and fills his pockets. Not in order to take them all away so I can be perfect, but because all these muddled, messy, miry bits of my life are the portals through which he can enter and make contact with me. And then he has to hurry off. So he can slip into your house too. And eventually he will set the clock going again and make it back into the burial garden just in time to see a young woman crying beside his empty tomb. Imagine that.

Part 15:

Sunday's Coming

Unrestrained

Zip over to Zephaniah 3 v 17 and you'll find the prophet assuring us that... '...the Lord your God is living among you. He is a mighty saviour. **He will take delight in you with gladness.** With his love, he will calm all your fears. **He will rejoice over you with joyful songs.**'

Rather exuberant and unrestrained don't you think. A God who leaves heaven so that he can wander these litter-strewn streets. And then start delighting in the likes of you and me, breaking into song every so often about us. Reminds me a little of the Lionesses invading that news conference and singing Football's Coming Home, one of them leaping on the interview desk to press home the point. I also think of the player who, in the middle of an interview on the pitch, upped and ran off with the microphone so she could join the rest of the team as they sang a full blooded, joy-bursting 'Sweet Caroline' with the crowd.

Resurrection

A man stands outside a tomb calling a name, the sun beats down, there's sound of mourning, and wailing, ululating fills the air around the grave. One day soon a tomb like this will be his and he won't stand outside of it, and no one will be calling his name, unless that is, he can hear the warm voice of his waiting father... but for now he is outside this tomb, and he is calling the name of his friend. With a kind of benevolent, gravelly urgency in his voice. The tracks of his tears still strain his face, his heart still feels a burden of grief. Beside him two sisters stand stark-eyed, their mouths open a little, unsure whether to be hopeful or terrified. There's a footstep and a cough and a groan and a splutter and then a bandaged figure steps into the sunlight looking for all the world as if he's a little lost. A rabbit in headlights, the brightest headlights in the universe. And the man who called his name steps forward and welcomes him back, unafraid of the strangeness of it all, unfazed by the regulations about physical contact with the dead. Are there rules about contact with the undead, or the till-quite-recently-dead? Who knows. He doesn't really care anyway. He's just embracing his friend, squeezing him tightly, then stepping back to give him room, and laughing while he unwraps his head bandages so the young man can squint once more into the sun, and into the faces of his aghast sisters. Something they all never thought he'd do again. Those beautiful eyes of his, alive once more, wide and drinking in the miracle of it all. His lungs inflating, breathing air again, his legs taking new steps, tottering like a toddler finding his feet for the first time.

And on a different Sunday morning there's an earthquake and the grating of a stone on the ground as it rolls away, and the sound of another footstep and another figure steps into the light, and it's as if the world breathes again and breaks into song after a deathly silence, as if creation has dawned once more, and the choir of angels who sang at his birth laugh and cheer and throw their halos in the air, as they celebrate in another realm that we call heaven. A realm which has now begun breaking and entering into this world. Like a thief in the night, and in the daytime too. A thief not come to rob and steal but a thief acting more like Father

Christmas, bringing good things, and leaving far more than he takes away.

Dark Morning

She wakes. Her eyes are dead. Seen too much murder disguised as punishment. She stands, washes, tries to convince herself it is worth getting up today. She spots the bundle by the door. Scoops it up, feels the weight and that shiver down her spine. Leaves the house and joins the shadows outside. Just another shadow moving amongst those etchings of moonlight. With every step her feet make a thud in the dirt. She's always been heavy footed, but this morning her walking sounds like a series of hammer blows. Thud. Another shiver down the spine. She had a dream once, it flashed through her mind when she felt a hand lift her out of the dirt. As she heard stones dropping her life raced before her eyes. It was a full life, a future suddenly bright. Hope transmitted in a stranger's smile. Now the dream lies in bits, like broken furniture in a room of arguments and bad memories. Thud. More steps. More shivers. She sees another shadow, fears the worst. But then the figure nods and the woman whispers. They walk on together, she's more aware than ever that her steps scuff and pound the earth. The other woman is so light on her feet, barely makes a sound.

Another shadow appears, and another. Soon there is a group of silent witnesses. Any other trip and they'd have been verbally elbowing each other out of the way to make conversation. But not here, not now. There's been little sleep amongst them, barely four hours between them. Their eyes all carry death in them. Preparing themselves for the sight they must confront. She presses the bundle closer to her body. One or two of the others have similar bundles. The garden. They stop, catch sight of the place in the moonlight. The ground shudders. She thinks at first it's lack of sleep. But the others clearly feel it too. There's a door stone lying loose and skewed, and a cave mouth yawning like an open dragon's den. Soldiers huddle nearby, they grunt and mutter. But they make no move towards the women. The women shuffle forward and look inside the dragon's mouth. There is no monster. But then… there is nothing at all. When they look outside they see the soldiers lying like corpses, faces pushed into the ground. Then the light hits them. A figure, dazzling as if lit by a thousand torches, sits astride the loose door stone. He speaks and his voice has the sound of a rushing river. Like a hundred shining figures. Phrases like 'been raised' 'was crucified' 'don't be afraid' 'not here' hang in the air like wisps of mist. The figure urges them into the cave. They look, but don't see, not yet. They turn and run, all their feet pounding heavily now, their bundles left behind, and the spark of life beginning to force the look of death from their eyes. Meanwhile one young woman hangs back.

Mary, Mary

She stands at the back of the room, a little miffed, it's fair to say. And she rolls her eyes. Just a little. So everyone's overjoyed now, are they? Leaping about, patting each other's backs. He's alive! they all say. He's back! Yay!

Sure. Everyone believes it now Peter's met him. Everyone's joining in now. Just one thing. She got there first, met him way before anyone else. But that wasn't good enough. Clearly. Couldn't possibly be true or real if it was only Mary who said so. But now Peter says it's happened, oh well, that's another story.

The sun is waning now, dipping well below the horizon, but it wasn't when she met him. It was barely awake then. A newly woken sun for a newly woken son.

And so Mary rolls her eyes. Later Paul will forget her too. Write about Peter's encounter, and James's, and a whole bunch of 500 nameless types, and yet somehow overlook the actual dawning of the new age. List a raft of encounters with that man from Galilee and yet omit the first witness to the bleary-eyed dawning moments.

(Many men paid little attention to the evidence of women in those days. Though we do know of one man who always paid attention to what women said.)

And so, with that in mind, let's go back to that encounter as the sun rose. A woman crying, sobbing her heart out, her head spinning and her stomach churning. And that gardener who calmed it all. Said her name and in doing so assured the world would come right once more. Mary. He didn't forget her, he didn't overlook her or miss her off the list. He set her at the very top. The first in line. The least turning out to be the most important for him. Mary. And as she ran to him, hurled herself at this resurrection man, she experienced what no one had experienced before, what billions have experienced since. The dawn of a new age in her heart and mind and strength and will. And the arrival in her life of an eternal friend. Jesus.

Creed

We believe in light,
And Jesus is his name.
We believe in peace,
And Jesus is his name.
We believe in meaning,
And Jesus is his name.

We believe in kindness,
And understanding,
We believe in forgiveness,
And Jesus is his name.

We believe in justice,
We believe in hope and freedom,
We believe in resurrection,
And Jesus is his name.

The Field

Let's not get stuck, whether we are full of faith, or full of questions, or full of both. Let's keep on learning, keep on digging for more. Keep asking, keep looking, keep knock-knock-knocking on heaven's door, keep searching for life's meaning and realties. Children are naturally curious. Let's get naturally curious too. Let's not settle for having found enough truth to get by, let's be benignly restless, divinely hungry. Others may not get it, you may be out front doing this, but don't give up. I read something profound recently, written by James Aladiran for the Lectio 365 app, about the guy in Jesus's parable in Matthew 13 verse 44. He would have looked crazy. He went out and spent everything on a field. Others around him, family, friends, strangers, enemies, may well have said that's a stupid idea. Why lay everything on the line for a field? Why go all out for a bit of turf? What they didn't know, couldn't see, was the treasure buried in the field. The man wasn't really just buying the field. He was after that treasure he'd discovered. You and I will go on discovering treasure from God, and others may only see the field. But there's always more treasure. In the world, in the Bible, in nature, in people, in conversations, in songs, in stories, in films, in encounters, in the ordinary, in science, in sport, in games, in listening, in pondering, in bantering, in dreams and daydreams, in the quiet, in the daylight, in the sun, the rain and the shadows. Always more treasure in those fields out there.

Part 16:
A Poem and a Play

Two extra pieces to end. One is a poem based on a piece of drama from years back, a story about the fears we have and the way they can entrap us. The other, *The Table*, is a longer piece inspired by a good friend.

The Land of Fear

Two went walking in the woods one spring,
With no idea what the walk might bring.
The girl fell asleep, near a big brown stone,
But the boy soon discovered they were not alone.

The stone was the rump of a big brown bear,
That reared its head and leered at him there.
He panicked and upped to the left and the right,
Ran back and forth in a frenzied fright.
The bear came close with his jagged smile,
Cornered him with his off-beat style:

'Hey slow down kid, tell me what you did,
That makes you rush and flip your lid.
I'm the boss round here, so lend an ear,
Why the frown and the frantic fear?
I'll teach you to dance, given half a chance,
I don't dig the way you move.

Better follow my way, or I'll spoil your day,
Come on boy, catch my groove.'

As he recoiled there, his head full of care,
The boy backed into a tree.
But it wasn't a tree, it hissed with glee,
A wild cat standing six foot three.

'Hey! You should come along with me,
I got a place that you should see.
You're clearly lost and lacking hope.
Are you some hero? ...er – nope!
Come on with me, let's go and eat,
It's been a while since I had meat.'

The boy was stuck and staring there,
A deer caught in a headlamp glare,
About to reply when what did he meet?
A speed freak knocked him right off his feet,
He scrambled up and scurrying there
Was a frazzled, stressed out, hurtling hare.

'Hello, goodbye, don't ask me why.
Keep moving now, don't stop somehow.
I've lost my hat, I've lost my coat,
I've lost my mind, I've lost my goat.
Say, have you seen... my magazine?

My toothbrush and my Windolene?
I know your face, I know that smile,
Weren't you once a crocodile?
D'you like my hat, d'you like my shoes?
Are you confused or just amused?
Panic, panic in your brain,
You may never be the same.
It's all too much, you'll never cope,
Why not give up and lose all hope?'

The cat kept prowling, the bear did too,
And the hare kept spinning in a right old stew.
And all seemed hopeless, all seemed gone,
The boy would never get back home.
And so he fell in a mound of tears,
And curled up there in a ball of fears.

'Why are you crying?' a calm voice said,
Strong and wise, as he lifted his head.
'The animals,' he muttered, 'there's no way home.'
'I know,' said the voice. *'But you're not alone.*
They've chased you for a good long while.
But I'm not afraid. I can help, my child.
I know the tricks of the big brown bear,
And the callous cat, and the stressful hare.
Let's meet them together, let me help you home,
I promise you – you're not alone.

175

I know those fears often cloud your mind,
And life for you is far from fine,
I'm on your side, I care for you too,
And I will never abandon you.'

The Table

From an idea by Paul Hobbs

Characters:

Mark Sand: a vicar in his late twenties.

Andy Fairbrother: 18, member of the local youth club.

Jack Freer: 57, hard-bitten coach of the local football team.

Trav, Giraffe, Dag, Spam, Pat, Mand & Jaz: local homeless folk of various ages.

Nick/Max: another homeless guy – feared by all the others.

Tim: 23, the goalkeeper in the local team.

Elle, Skylar & Vicky: twenties, WAGs of the football team.

Stephen & Judy: a married couple in their thirties.

Geraldine: 20, a friend of Andy's.

- - -

Scene 1. Mark Sand's study.

Mark sits at his desk, the thing is untidy as hell, books and papers strewn across the surface. He picks up his phone, jabs at numbers and speaks.

'Hello? Hello... yes, yes that's right. Mark Sand, yea that's it, Reverend Sand, that's right, vicar of All Saints. I er... I was wondering if you rent out cutlery? Yes, silver if possible. For twelve, no, thirteen actually. Yes, I know, that's been my problem.'

He smiles as he listens then goes on.

'You do? Place settings – for thirteen? Excellent. Well, I think I'll need them for a week, better say two to be safe. I can come in tomorrow? Is that okay? 13 Wilmot Drive. Thank you.'

Mark gives his number then hangs up without saying goodbye, the way no one seems to ever say goodbye in stories. He sits back in his chair. He nods to himself as he thinks for a few seconds before reaching for a notepad and pencil. The pad's a wad of used pages stapled together so the blank sides show up for writing on. He pulls off a sheet and starts scribbling, his handwriting is a lilting mess.

Mark mutters to himself.

'Right. Let's think. The football club, if we make that Tuesday, the park on Wednesday, the gallery on Friday, and here for Sunday. Hmm. Should do it. Now... the small matter of a table...'

He reaches for the phone again.

Scene 2. Beside the pitch at the local football club.

Jack Freer, the club's coach smokes as he chats with Mark. They're watching a bedraggled team jog round the pitch.

Jack sighs. 'Tuesday? Could be difficult, after all the lads have got a tough season coming up. Away match next

Saturday, I don't know how they'd take the break in routine.'

Mark offers a smile. 'Looks to me as if they'd welcome the change.'

Jack's not amused and he looks Mark up and down.

Jack counters, 'All Saints church you said? Yea, my ex was none too happy with your lot. You can be awkward buggers can't ya?'

Mark looks apologetic. 'I'm sorry, I wouldn't know, I've only been here a few months.'

Jack says, 'Oh aye, new boy, eh? Fresh out of some high–flying ecclesiastical place? Coming here trying to impress us heathen eh. Damn funny idea anyway, isn't it?'

'I'm from Brixton, actually. Do you know it?' Mark asks him.

Jack stares at him. 'Tuesday, you said? Well... I'll see what I can do... but I'm not promising.'

He turns and shouts at the players. 'Get them bloody legs up, Smith, and stop all that panting, Wells, you're like bloody Darth Vader!'

Mark's walking away when Jack calls out.

Jack calls after him. 'Eh, mind you, we haven't got a table anything like as big as you want.'

Mark calls back, 'Oh that's no bother, I'm bringing my own.'

Jack frowns. 'Bringing your... what's all this in aid of?'

Mark shrugs, throwing up both hands. 'Oh... call it... experience.'

179

'Experience?'

'Yea. Experiential learning.'

Jack shakes his head. 'What the bloody hell's that?'

Mark says, 'Tuesday... you'll see, Goodbye Mr Freer.'

Jack turns away with a sigh. 'Ought to get himself a proper job. Smith! Knees! Wells! Shut it!'

Scene 3. The park.

Mark sits on a bench with his back to the busy main road, throwing crumbs to the pigeons. He glances around. There's a homeless guy lying splayed on the grass, a bottle in one hand. He's staring at Mark.

Mark asks him, 'You all right?'

The homeless guy ignores this and turns his body away.

Mark gets up and saunters over, he flops down on the grass, it's a bit on the damp side.

Mark tries again. 'Hi there. My name's Mark. What's happening? How you doing?'

Trav grunts. 'How's it look like I'm doing?'

Mark shrugs. 'Well, I dunno, you tell me.'

'Are you some social worker or park official come to kick me out?' snaps Trav, 'cause you won't do it. They tried it before.'

'Who did?'

'The council, who d'you think?'

Mark presses on. 'D'you have anywhere to live?'

'Doubt it. What do you think? I'm out here because I got a tasty little manor, tucked away in the country? Yea, I only come to the city for the business, ya know. Oh here he comes! You want to make light conversation? Try Giraffe here, he really graduated well in the university of life. Didn't ya, Giraffe?'

The lean figure comes over, sits down.

Giraffe mutters at them. 'Have you seen him? Have you? He was after me again.'

He disappears behind a bush.

Trav taps his temple. 'Complete screwball, he is. Radio ga ga.'

Mark laughs. 'And you're not? And I'm not?'

Trav sneers at him. 'Do me a favour! Alright, this wasn't exactly my lifelong ambition, but it's kept me sane. Giraffe, come out you prat.'

Giraffe's head pops up from behind the bush and peers around looking for all the world like a meerkat.

Giraffe says, 'Dogs now. They've got dogs.'

He takes a chance on it and rushes over and crashes his long body on the grass, colliding with Mark as he lands.

Giraffe says again, 'They got dogs you know!'

Trav is not impressed. 'Yea, yea, and sabre-tooth tigers no doubt an' all.'

Mark says, 'Hi Giraffe my name's Mark, what are you frightened of?'

Giraffe looks startled, flicks his head from Mark to Jack and back again.

Giraffe says, 'Him! It's him. He's come!'

Trav says, 'Shut up! Jerk!'

Giraffe persists though. 'Isn't it him?'

Trav rolls his eyes. 'No! You're a complete sandwich short of a sixpence, Giraffe, this geezer wants a chat, humour him will ya? Tell him about the bad men... and the nasty women.'

Trav stands up and stretches.

Giraffe nods at the bottle he's left behind on the grass. 'Trav, can I have that?'

Trav shrugs. 'It's empty, mate.'

Giraffe nods. 'It'll be exactly what I need though.'

Trav hands him the bottle, Mark recoils a little, for fear he might get hit with the thing.

Trav spits on his hands and wipes them on his coat, then he spits again and rubs his face.

Trav says, 'Gotta go, got an appointment.'

He starts to walk away.

Mark calls out, 'I'm having a bit of a do, next Wednesday, wanna come?'

Trav stops and looks back, he looks around.

'You talking to me?' he says.

Giraffe says, 'I'll come! As long as they leave the dogs locked up.'

Trav agrees. 'Yea, have Lofty here instead, he's more entertaining.'

Mark says, 'I want you both, and them other two chaps that were here yesterday.'

Trav laughs. 'You're kidding. Jed and Pete? They're headcases. At least Giraffe's harmless. He smells like cat's puke but he ain't hurt anyone.'

Mark keeps on. 'Jed and Pete – will you tell 'em?'

Trav says, 'Tell 'em what?'

Mark leaps up and walks over to Trav and puts a hand on his shoulder.

Mark says, 'Next Wednesday night here in the park, I'm having a do. Top class meal, no riff raff, all for you guys.'

Trav frowns. 'Are you Bob Geldof or something?'

Mark smiles. 'Will you come?'

Trav shrugs. 'Won't have to come – I'll be here won't I. So will Jed and Lofty and Spam and Dag... and a dozen more. You wanna watch your back coming here with them ideas.'

Mark says, 'So I can do it?'

Trav fires back, 'Do what you like, guv, it's a free country... that's what they told me at borstal anyway...'

Trav walks away, limping slightly on his left foot. He flexes his shoulders as if he's about to enter a boxing ring. Giraffe clambers up to Mark and grabs his hand, he nods repeatedly and grins at Mark. Mark smiles and shakes his hand. But when he tries to let go Lofty hangs on, still nodding and grinning. Mark walks away with Lofty still hanging on.

Scene 4. Inside the "Craftsman" Art Gallery.

Mark meets a lively, elderly woman, and they start discussing details of using the gallery for a meal. The walls are lined with paintings, and there are also several wooden sculptures on stands, piles of bricks, and tables. At the end of their conversation the woman takes a card from a nearby table and hands it to Mark. He reads it and nods, they then examine the carpet together, Mark rubs his hand over it. The woman looks worried, but Mark seems reassured. They walk to the door together, he shakes her hand and they say goodbye.

Scene 5. Mark's study.

Mark's typing invitations, one finger at a time. It's an understandably slow process but he's well used to it. He's typed all sorts like this, funeral services, wedding services, baptism services. Services mostly. The phone rings. Mark looks at it and answers it.

'Hello, Mark Sand. Yea, hi Andy.'

He relaxes back in his chair and stretches.

'So – what's the news? The table? You've got it! Excellent! How much? How much!! Okay, okay, it's alright, we can't do it without it. So – tomorrow night at the football ground. 6.30 okay? Yea, it's all set. See you there.'

Mark hangs up and sits thinking. Slowly he smiles to himself. He closes his eyes and bows his head. Then he looks up again, stares at the typos on the invitations on the screen and presses delete a few times.

Scene 6. The bar at the local football ground.

In the middle of the room there's a large battered wooden table, surrounded by chairs. Mark is leaning against the bar talking to Jack Freer. Andy Fairbrother, Mark's friend, throws out the table cloth with an attempted flourish. The cloth is white and crisp, and easily covers the table. Mark holds up a menu and starts reading it out.

Mark reads out, 'Chicken and mushroom soup with croutons and lashings of cream; steak and Guinness casserole, with creamed potatoes, carrots, courgettes and dumplings; sherry trifle, apple pie and cream or black forest gateau to finish. All washed down with a bottle of red wine. How's that sound?'

Jack is unimpressed. 'Well, it'll do, but listen, son, I'm trying to tell ya – they're not all coming.'

Mark says, 'Sorry?'

Jack tells him, 'The lads. I did my best, just like I said.'

Mark can't believe it. 'They couldn't come to a free meal? Don't they like a bit of a do?'

Jack throws up his hands. 'Oh, yea, I'll say! Can't keep 'em away... normally, only – well, this is different, son.'

Mark says, 'In what way?'

Jack thinks for a moment. 'Well... you. They ain't used to going out with a vicar.'

'I don't want to go out with them I want to give 'em a good meal.'

'Yea, but they don't know you.'

Mark nods. 'Exactly.'

He gestures in the direction of the table. Andy is laying out the cutlery and glasses for 13 places.

Mark says, 'This is the perfect opportunity. To get to know me.'

Jack frowns. 'Is that what this is then son, a recruitment drive for the church?'

Mark shakes his head. 'No. Actually it isn't. That's just what it isn't. I wanted to share a meal with them. That's all.'

Jack says, 'Yea, well, folks don't do that, do they? Not when you don't know 'em from Adam.'

Mark narrows his eyes a little as he looks at Jack and starts shaking his head. He sighs and walks away.

Mark sighs. 'Andy, I think you'd better pack up.'

Jack stops him. 'Hang on there, son, hang on, hang on, you can't do that. I got people coming, people after a good feed.'

At that moment three women in their twenties appear in the doorway, they're heavily made up, dressed in tight dresses and high heels.

Elle says, 'Jack, we're here! Where's the party?'

Jack looks at Mark and raises his eyebrows. 'I said the lads wouldn't all come – but I got contacts, you know, a man with my influence. I got ten of the club's wags here.

Oh yea, and the goalkeeper. He said he'd come when I told him who else I'd invited.'

A whole group of women starts piling through the door, all chatting, vaping and laughing together. The goalkeeper wanders in behind them, looking awkward and not a little edgy.

Jack announces, 'Right, folks, grab a seat, this lad's the vicar, that's his assistant, and the hot pot's coming right up.'

Jack throws an arm around the goalkeeper.

'Tim! Don't look so worried!'

There's the sound of scraping chairs as they all grab seats, the food is served up and they start eating. Andy hovers around with the wine while Mark takes care of the food. Half an hour slips by and the goalkeeper forgets his worries as he and the others tuck in.

Elle calls out, 'Hey vicar I didn't know you sort o' dudes could cook?'

Skylar says, 'Yea, this is a nice spread.'

She winks at Vicky and says, 'Wonder what else he can do?'

The others hear this and there is a splutter of laughter.

Mark is unfazed. 'Well, I have to admit – I didn't do all this myself.'

Vicky says, 'Oh yea? Got a lady friend somewhere, have you?'

Mark grins, 'Several – and they're all over sixty.'

There is more laughter.

Skylar says, 'Come on, vic, when you gonna sit down and eat.'

She pats the empty seat next to her.

Skylar says, 'It'll all be gone if you wait too long.'

Mark refuses. 'No, I'm not eating myself.'

The room falls silent as they all look at him.

Skylar says quietly, 'But there's a spare place here. Come on, sit down, there's loads of food.'

Mark sticks to his guns. 'Well, Andy and I are dishing up – we didn't come to eat.'

Elle says, 'Well then... why did you come?'

Mark smiles. 'For the meal, for you...'

The others look perplexed.

Jack says, 'You may as well have this spare seat, son.'

Mark says, 'It's not spare.'

They all look over at the thirteenth place, next to Skylar. She lifts the cloth and peers under the table.

Vicky chips in, 'He's frightened of sitting next to you, Skylar, that's what it is really!'

Mark replies hastily, 'Of course not!'

He pauses and wipes his hands on a cloth.

'That place is for someone else. This meal is a sort of celebration for them.'

Elle says, 'Well, they'd better get a move on or they'll be celebrating empty plates!'

Mark smiles, and he glances at Andy.

Mark says, I'm sorry... I'm not quite sure what to do now.'

Skylar suggests, 'How about the pudding?'

That breaks the tension and Mark laughs.

'Good idea, Andy dish up the afters and I'll read 'em something.'

He looks round the table at the others.

Mark asks, 'Is that alright? You eat, I'll read?'

Elle says, 'Not 50 Shades is it?'

And they all laugh. Gateau, pie and trifle are brought out and plonked on the table. Mark flips through a black Bible. There is general chatting again, as they all pile into the food.

Mark starts reading. 'When the hour came, Jesus and his twelve disciples sat eating at the table. He said to everyone: "I have really looked forward to having this meal with you".'

Mark glances up, some are eating or chatting, but most are listening.

Mark reads on. 'Then Jesus took some bread, gave thanks for it and broke it up. He said: "This is my body, broken for you, and this cup of wine is my blood, poured out for you."'

Mark looks up again, there is silence now. Everyone is staring at him, some with quizzical looks. Eventually Jack clears his throat and gets up.

Jack says, 'Yes, well, that was very nice of you, vicar. That was a grand meal, I'm sure. You're very generous. Yea, very generous... cheers mate.'

He picks up his jacket, and shakes Mark's hand, which is a little awkward due to him holding the large Bible. And then he walks out. Several of the others continue eating slowly.

Vicky says suddenly. 'Stink! Is that the time? Sorry vicar. I've gotta go, I said I'd be... well, meet someone, you know. Elle, you coming?'

Elle looks at Mark. 'Yea, yea, sorry, I think I'd better go too. Me old mum's at home... ya know... I told her I wouldn't be late.'

Several others get up and leave. Mark sits in a vacated chair and watches them go. Andy appears with more wine.

Andy says, 'Anyone for another slurp?'

He offers it to silent refusals. The rest of the group leave, some of them looking a bit thrown by things. Only Tim the goalkeeper is left.

Tim chirps, 'Well, that was a clever move, wasn't it, Rev? You know how to clear a room.'

He nods at the Bible.

Mark shrugs. 'You're the keeper right? Brave man with all these women.'

Tim laughs. Why d'you do it? The meal – why d'you do all this?'

Mark says, 'Why d'you think I did it?'

Tim looks down the empty table then back at Mark – "cause you're a bloody fool I guess.'

Mark nods. 'Okay then. Yea, 'cause I'm a bloody fool.'

Tim laughs again and shakes his head. 'Give us another top up will ya, I'm in no hurry, sit down and have a glass with me. I think you're the brave man you know…'

Andy fills a glass for Mark and tops up Tim's, the three of them sit together.

Scene 7. The park.

It is early evening, beginning to grow dark. The wooden table is set on the grass, Andy sets out the cutlery on the cloth which is now creased and stained. A few yards away a group of homeless folks are sitting on the grass. They are watching Andy with amusement. Occasionally calling out. A car pulls up on the other side of the fence. Mark hops out and pulls a large bowl from the boot. It's covered with a cloth. He carries it slowly through the gate and to the table.

Mark says, 'Well done, Trav! I see you kept your part of the deal.'

Trav mutters back, 'I done nothing! I told you – we live here anyway. You wanna have a knees–up it's your lookout.'

The others look at Trav. He shrugs, takes a swig from his can, and looks away.

Mark puts the bowl down on the table and rubs his hands. 'There! Well done, Andy. Get the wine from the boot will you?'

He turns to the crowd on the grass.

Mark announces, 'Right! Here it is, lads. Get it while it's hot.'

The group stares at him without moving. He holds out his hand to the table

Mark says, 'It's all yours.'

Mark grabs a bottle and starts to uncork it. The bunch on the grass still haven't moved.

Mark says, 'Oh, you can sit anywhere, you know. Don't wait to be told. Twelve free places, booked and paid for. Stew, dumplings, wine, rolls... What's wrong? Aren't you hungry? Look, I'm not joking.'

He dips a finger in the stew, yanks it back out and quickly recoils, sucking his finger.

'Ow! It's hot! Mmm... and delicious!'

He pours a glass of wine. Then another. The bunch are still quiet and staring. Mark looks from one face to the next. He stops at Trav.

Mark pleads, 'Trav? Help me out, will you, it's getting cold.'

Trav looks away.

Mark says, 'Giraffe?'

Mark walks over and grabs Giraffe's hand. Giraffe looks up and grins. Mark looks at Andy helplessly.

Mark says, 'Well, don't any of you want some food? Grief, I don't believe this! Look!'

He picks up a ladle of steaming stew.

'It's hot food – free!'

He offers a glass of wine to the group, they frown and look away. Mark puts it down and goes up to Andy.

Mark whispers, 'Andy, I'm going to ask you to do something, okay? They're all shy, or terrified, or something. Sit down and start eating will you?'

Andy frowns. 'I dunno…'

Mark urges him, 'If you make a start it might encourage the others.'

Andy says, 'I'm sorry, I really want to help but I'd feel a bit of an idiot. You know, out here, eating on my own… and I had something before I came out.'

Mark looks down at the grass, and kicks at the ground, frustration simmering.

Mark says, 'Okay. Okay, don't worry. Andy, you take the bottle and pour out twelve glasses – I'm going to eat something.'

Mark walks past the others and sits at the head of the table. He piles some stew on his plate and starts eating. He looks at Lofty and nods. Lofty is licking his lips.

Mark says with his mouth full, 'It's good. Very good. Whenever you guys are ready.'

He raises his glass to drink, then a voice bellows at them, from across the park.

Nick calls out, 'What the soddin' hell's going on here?'

Nick strides across to them, all trench coat, bad teeth and broad shoulders. Trav grins and looks at Mark.

Trav looks at Mark. 'You're in trouble now.'

Mark looks worried, 'What? Why?'

Trav says, 'It's Nick! Only we call him, Max – 'cause he's mad!'

Nick steps up close to Mark at the table, leering down at him.

Nick booms, 'What's this friggin' thing doing in our soddin' park? I'll rip your grinning face off mate.'

Mark clears his throat and wipes his mouth with the back of his hand. He stands and holds out his hand.

'Hi... I er... my name's Mark... Who are you?'

Nick glares at his outstretched hand. 'Who am I? Who am I?'

Mark presses on, 'Er... yes... I'm Mark. What's yours... your name I mean?'

Nick looks round, the others are watching closely.

Nick mutters, 'Yea! Well, yea. I'm er, you know... Max... but you can call me Nick, see...'

Mark nods. 'I'm very pleased to meet you, Nick.'

Nick looks confused. 'Yea, Nick, that's my name, only these scum never use it.'

He spits the words out at the others.

Mark asks him, 'Would you like something to eat, Max... er Nick, or a drink?'

Nick looks at the table. 'This all yours then?'

Mark says, 'Yea. Well, no. Not exactly. It's yours. I brought it here for you lot.'

Nick looks at the glass of wine.

Mark says, 'We're trying to give it away, but no one wants it. Do you want it, Nick? We got stew and cake and pudding. It's all here.'

Nick holds up the flat of his hand, Mark stops. Nick looks at the table, then turns on the others.

Nick barks at them, 'What you soddin' lot staring at? You heard the geezer, there's food here for you.'

They still stare.

Nick says, 'Well... d'ya want it or don't ya?'

Giraffe stumbles to his feet and walks a few steps. Nick grabs him and pulls him over.

Nick says, 'There you go, Giraffe – there ain't no dogs here! Dive in.'

Giraffe grabs a chair. He pulls over the plate of stew Mark had served up for himself and starts eating rapidly.

Nick is now moving about amongst the others.

He says, 'Dag! Pat! Jaz! Spam! Get over there. Now!'

Nick pushes the others towards the table. They look at one another then stumble across and start eating. Mark walks up to Trav. He is sitting alone now, looking away.

Mark says, 'Trav, come on, please. Join us. Not 'cause of Mad Max – 'cause I'm asking you.'

Trav turns and looks at Mark. 'You don't half fancy yourself as Bob Geldof, don't ya?'

Mark smiles. 'Maybe. Maybe that's why I'm here, I don't know. I just don't want you to miss out.'

Slowly Trav stands and tosses his can to Mark who catches it awkwardly.

Trav says, 'Who's missing out?'

He strolls to the table and eases into a seat. Mark looks across at Andy and nods. The table is now full apart from the seat next to Trav. Nick is about to sit down there when Mark sees this and runs over.

Mark says, 'Ah! Nick! Nick, not there. Sorry – it's a spare place.'

Nick says, 'Yea, I know – for me!'

Mark says, 'Well, not exactly no.'

Nick insists, 'Yea. It's for me. I'm tellin' you, aren't I?'

Mark tells him, 'Look, it isn't for you, okay? Not at all.'

Nick stares at Mark. There is an awkward silence.

Mark says, 'Listen... Trav. Help us get the food will you? Only we need a hand, and... well, Nick here needs a seat.'

Trav looks at Nick, sighs, then gets up. Mark pats his shoulder. Nick sits down. Everyone rapidly devours the food, with plenty of belching, squelching and sniffing. Trav and Andy have their work cut out keeping up.

Trav pulls Andy aside. 'What's your guvnor up to?'

Andy says, 'You'll see. Here, I found this dumpling...'

He hands over a soggy piece of suet and Trav swallows it down and grins.

Andy winces. 'No I meant... I found it on the grass!'

Trav shrugs. 'Huh... what's new? Just like momma used to make...'

Standing at the table behind the empty chair, Mark is holding his Bible.

Mark says, 'I don't want to interrupt so please don't feel you have to stop eating.'

They ignore this.

Mark goes on. 'I just want to read you something...' (He opens the book) 'When the hour came, Jesus and his twelve disciples sat eating at the table.' (The noisy eating continues) 'Jesus said: "I have looked forward to eating this meal with... you..." then...' (Mark hesitates) '...then he took some...' (He looks up. They are totally oblivious to him. He glances round slowly from face to face, then looks at his Bible and turns back a few pages. He looks across to Trav and Andy then reads:) 'A man was holding a luxurious banquet, with rich food and fine wines. But the guests he invited refused to come, so he said to his servant, "Go out to the streets of the town, and bring back the poor, the crippled, the blind and the lame – as many as you can find." So...'

Mark looks up at the guests round the table. He smiles as he reads on.

'So the servant went out and brought them all into the master's house.'

One or two of the group look up, smile at Mark and nod, then return to their eating.

Scene 8. The Craftsman Art Gallery.

The room is completely silent, the table is laid for 13 and the cloth is very badly stained now. Andy is sitting at one end of the table, Mark at the other. They look at each other. Mark checks his watch.

Andy says, 'A few more minutes, eh? Just a bit longer... it's worth the wait.'

Mark sighs. He taps his fingers on a dark ragged patch on the table cloth. There is silence.

Andy looks at the cloth. 'This is in a bad way, mate. I mean – it's seen some action this week, hasn't it? I'm not entirely sure that it was really ready for it.'

They both check their watches.

Andy sighs, 'Ah well – can't please all the people all the time, can ya?'

He reaches out for a sheet of paper which is lying on the table.

Andy says, 'I mean, you were aiming a bit high... These guys are practically royalty. Danny Short? That guy hasn't been in church since he crawled out of nappies. And John Fleet, well, he buys and sells churches in his spare time – and at a tidy profit. Doubt if he ever bothers to stick his head inside one.'

Mark sighs and shifts position in his chair.

Andy says, 'Give yourself a break, eh?'

Mark replies, 'Andy, I didn't invite these people to a church. For goodness sake! They all look at art, don't they? They all like good food, don't they?'

Andy says, 'Yea... but maybe they're all vegetarians... or maybe they're frightened.'

Mark frowns. 'Frightened?'

Andy says, 'They don't know you.'

Mark says, 'I took Danny's father's funeral.'

'Oh! Did you? Maybe he forgot. He was probably too emotional to remember you.'

'Perhaps he was. I do seem to recall him having one or two drinks afterwards. Still, that's what it's all about, isn't it?'

Andy says, 'What do you mean?'

Mark says, 'Well, we still held our meal, didn't we? Just because we didn't have any guests it doesn't mean it wasn't a success.'

Andy looks confused. 'I don't follow that, Mark.'

'Well, you can have a party where everyone turns up – and yet it still turns out to be a complete disaster. So perhaps it's actually possible to have a dinner that is more successful without its guests? Or maybe Tim was right. Perhaps I am just a complete idiot.'

He screws up a menu and throws it across the table.

Mark goes on. 'But I'll tell you something – I bet you there's one guest who didn't refuse the invitation.'

He looks at the thirteenth place.

Andy shakes his head and stands up. 'Come on, vicar, I'll buy you a drink. We can clear this lot up later... When we're both paralytic...'

Mark looks at him, eyes wide. Andy grins.

Andy says, 'Only kidding!'

They both walk out.

Scene 9. Mark's vicarage.

The table is now standing in the centre of Mark's dining room, loaded with food. It's still decked with the same cloth, still extremely soiled. Mark, Andy and three other guests, Geraldine, Stephen and Judy, are standing around it, drinks in hand, staring at the food. They are all part of Mark's congregation.

Stephen frowns. 'Did you really have to bring this monstrosity in here? Look at the state of it!'

Judy agrees. 'I'm surprised you didn't give yourselves a hernia.'

Andy says, 'We nearly did, believe me!'

Geraldine says, 'If you don't mind me asking, Mark... well... why did you do it? What was it all in aid of?'

Mark reaches over for one of the sandwiches that no one else is eating.

Mark asks, 'Do what, Geraldine?'

Stephen snaps, 'Oh come on, Mark, you know perfectly well what she means. All this business with the tramps. I mean look at it... I mean... well... look at it... it's... well look at it!'

Mark is nonplussed. 'Perhaps I did it just to see if it could be done – like climbing Everest!'

Mark and Andy laugh. The others don't. So Mark sighs.

'For goodness sake – it was an experiment, an idea! That's all.'

Judy says, 'And I suppose we're to be the final part of that?'

Mark says, 'Yes. Now that you put it that way, yes. You see I wanted...'

Stephen interrupts him. 'I beg your pardon?'

Andy says, 'Well, Mark had this idea of a table for twelve, bit like the last supper, except different and sharing it with four different groups... a way of introducing them to... well a way of...'

Stephen places his glass delicately on the table, doing his best to avoid the crusty splodges and marks.

Stephen says coldly. 'I see. So we are just part four of your little theological experiment after the soccer hooligans, tramps and thieves?'

Andy corrects him. 'Thieves? No, part three was an art gallery...'

Stephen snaps back. 'I don't care if it was the Louvre! This all seems a bloody far cry from what the church should be doing! And when you invited us here tonight, Mark Sand, you said nothing about any damn experiment. I won't be humiliated like this, I won't. And please... don't try and explain. You've done enough of that.'

He grabs his coat and walks out. Judy looks apologetic and hastily follows him. There's an embarrassed silence.

Geraldine says quietly, 'Well, it does all seem a little odd, Mark. And people have been talking, word travels you know. The local papers'll have a field day.'

Mark says, 'Good!'

He pulls out a chair and takes a seat.

Geraldine says, 'You can't mean that?'

Mark replies, 'Well, at least they'll be giving other people a rest if they're writing about me! Frankly, I don't care. I've spent the last seven days working my backside off just so that I can be snubbed and insulted by four different layers of society. After the flack I've endured this week the worst the press can do is spell my name wrong! Now... (He snatches up his Bible) I have faithfully finished each meal this week with the word of God. Are you staying for it – or would you prefer EastEnders?'

Geraldine says, 'Mark, I'm sorry. I... I've had quite enough of all this... it's confusing. It makes no sense... It's not right...'

She leaves, shaking her head. Andy pulls up a seat and sits opposite Mark.

Andy grimaces. 'All that food wasted again.'

Mark smiles at him. 'At least you came Andy.'

Andy nods. 'Yea. Nowhere else to go mate. This is where it's happening.'

He smiles.

Mark picks up his Bible and reads from it. 'Behold...' (He hesitates) 'Behold I stand at the door and knock... if anyone hears my voice and opens the door I will come

202

into his house and eat with him...' (He closes the book) 'and he will eat with me...'

They both look at the empty seats and then stare at the food laid out on the table.

Some of the writing that has inspired me:

Who Moved the Stone: Frank Morison

BRF Book of 365 Reflections: especially p88 Debbie Orris

Paul the Traveller: Ernle Bradford

What is the Bible: Rob Bell

Velvet Elvis: Rob Bell

What We Talk About When We Talk About God: Rob Bell

The New Testament for Everyone: Tom Wright

The Badly Behaved Bible: Nick Page

The Wrong Messiah: Nick Page

Eat This Book: Eugene Peterson

Alabaster: Chris Aslan

Manacle: Chris Aslan

Mosaic: Chris Aslan

Jesus Through Middle Eastern Eyes: Kenneth Bailey

Journeying with Jonah: Denis McBride

The Bible Project videos on YouTube

Printed in Great Britain
by Amazon

12701716R00119